Key Decisions in U.S. History

A PARTICIPATORY APPROACH

Volume 2

1861–1994

———————————— Reproducible Teacher Book ————————————

Patrick Henry Smith and John Croes

J. WESTON

WALCH

PUBLISHER

Portland, Maine

User's Guide
to
Walch Reproducible Books

As part of our general effort to provide educational materials which are as practical and economical as possible, we have designated this publication a "reproducible book." The designation means that purchase of the book includes purchase of the right to limited reproduction of all pages on which this symbol appears:

Here is the basic Walch policy: We grant to individual purchasers of this book the right to make sufficient copies of reproducible pages for use by all students of a single teacher. This permission is limited to a single teacher, and does not apply to entire schools or school systems, so institutions purchasing the book should pass the permission on to a single teacher. Copying of the book or its parts for resale is prohibited.

Any questions regarding this policy or requests to purchase further reproduction rights should be addressed to:

Permissions Editor
J. Weston Walch, Publisher
321 Valley Street • P. O. Box 658
Portland, Maine 04104-0658

1   2   3   4   5   6   7   8   9   10
ISBN 0-8251-3325-4

Copyright © 1997
J. Weston Walch, Publisher
P. O. Box 658 • Portland, Maine 04104-0658
Printed in the United States of America

Contents

Acknowledgments

This book was eight years in the making. Conceived during a most rewarding year of team teaching at Lowell High School in Massachusetts, the project was interrupted by Patrick Henry Smith's move to Mexico. In our working visits between the United States and Mexico, and in our research, preparation, and communications, many people in both countries have helped us.

Without the use of the Internet, available through the University of Massachusetts/Lowell's connection with Lowell High School, the project would still be far from complete. Richard Coffey, Pat Grucca, Dave Faxon, René Méndez, Monica Vázquez, the United Teachers of Lowell, and Yuhsi Takahashi have our sincere gratitude for their time and efforts on our behalf.

The staff at the Littlefield Library in Tyngsboro, Massachusetts, was very helpful in acquiring books and assisting with research. In Scottsdale, Arizona; Bowdoinham, Maine; Washington, D.C.; and Cholula, Mexico, Louise and Craig Salminen, Carl Smith, and Karen Tilbor, K.L. Smith, and Chris Hall made our work possible.

We have used these materials with many of our classes, and we have offered them to other teachers to try out. Louis Pauls, Sofia San Millan, Maribeth O'Neil, David Kertzner, Maura Ammendolia, Kim Parent, Dean Bergeron, Ann Bassett, John Moore, Bill McDonnell, Hung Nguyen, Art Hamilton, and especially Miriam Morgenstern have given us important feedback and shown us many new ways of using these decisions. To all the students who have decided their way through history with us and given their feedback, and to the teachers who have helped us refine the lessons, we are indebted. Most appreciated, too, have been the close reading and professional advice provided by the editors at J. Weston Walch: Lisa French, Richard Kimball, Julie Mazur, and Pam O'Neil.

We thank our families for giving us the time and support we needed to write this book. Patricia A. Ryan, most valued fellow teacher and wife, despite forfeiting her husband to countless hours and even a Christmas vacation of writing and revising, has patiently and dependably provided unflagging support and honest, constructive, and much appreciated advice that was, as always, right. Hilda Rodriguez found time to listen and laugh and to do more than her fair share of child care while finishing a law degree. Arantza Smith-Rodriguez, who came along in the middle of the project, kindly slept through late nights of typing and printing. Without their support, we could not have written this book.

Final acknowledgments go to Abraham Lincoln, Frederick Douglass, Davy Crockett, Crazy Horse, Randy Stakeman, and untold others for inspiring and fascinating us with history in the first place.

Patrick H. Smith
Universidad de las
   Américas-Puebla
Cholula, Mexico;
University of Arizona

John Croes
Lowell High School
Lowell, Massachusetts

Credits

Dover Pictorial Archive

Pages 3, 7, 9, 11, 13, 21, 33, 47, 70

North Wind Picture Archives

Pages 1, 35

Corel Professional Photos

Pages 15, 95

Rubberball Productions

Page 95

Library of Congress

Page 17, LC-USZ62-107756

AP/Wide World Photos

Pages 27, 43, 51, 57, 59, 61, 63, 67, 69, 71, 93, 97

Archives of the Franciscan Province of the Sacred Heart

Page 29

Corbis-Bettmann

Pages 37, 39, 50, 55, 65, 73, 80, 105

Introduction

History is stories. It is stories about people engaged with the events, ideas, environment, and people of their times. History is people making decisions about their lives. Nothing had to happen the way it did. If people had decided differently, stories would be different. It was the decisions that made the stories. Our approach to teaching history is to involve students in the issues and decisions that people have faced. By making those decisions themselves, our students sense the urgency and emotions present in the times and people they are learning about. We have yet to find a student "Bostonian" who did not demand to throw the British tea into the harbor. Likewise, our student "colonial governors" are ready to punish those Boston rabble-rousers.

Why we wrote *Key Decisions*

We wrote *Key Decisions in U.S. History*, Volumes 1 and 2, to enable students to better comprehend U.S. history classes. As teachers in a transitional bilingual education program, we experimented with different textbooks and discovered that despite our students' ability to decode written text, many were unable to comprehend the historical events described in the textbook. We believe this difficulty is often rooted in a lack of schema, or previous knowledge, to employ when reading history. Even the best organized and most clearly written textbook may be incomprehensible to students who have little background knowledge. We wrote *Key Decisions* to provide the preliminary schema necessary to read history.

We also wrote history in a decisions format because it is a powerful and practical way to involve students in the urgency and emotions of historical events and to foster perspective. As Gerald Horne wrote in *Thinking and Rethinking U.S. History*, "If students are given the information necessary to comprehend another national perspective on past events, it can help them search for and understand other nations' perspectives on current events." (p. 209) However, we want our students not only to comprehend different perspectives but also to act on

them by making decisions. And to encourage decision making that is as informed as possible, we provide adequate background information that is readable but not simplistic. Although the language has been simplified, the issues have not. In fact, our vignettes often provide more detailed information on particular incidents than many texts do because we are asking students to make informed decisions.

What *Key Decisions* is and is not

Key Decisions in U.S. History is not a comprehensive history text and does not cover all the events that history texts do. Rather, it is a supplement that helps students understand some of the events in any U.S. history text. Besides leading to better understanding of the main text, *Key Decisions* helps students to become more actively involved in the class and to appreciate how historical events result from realistic decisions made by real or realistic people.

Who *Key Decisions* is for

Key Decisions is written for teachers and students of U.S. history. We have used these decisions mostly with high school students in ESL/sheltered English history courses, but they can be used with any students reading English at the intermediate (fourth- to eighth-grade) level, including those in junior high and senior high, adult education, and citizenship courses. *Key Decisions* does not assume or require any prior knowledge or study of U.S. history. Each vignette (or series of vignettes, in some cases) presents all the information a student needs to make the decision. Some vignettes build on or contrast with others, but information from other resources is not needed in order to make these decisions. The decision format readily incorporates the knowledge, skills, and opinions that students bring to the lessons, a useful feature in heterogeneous groupings. Because students bring their different points of view—as male or female, as black, white, Asian, Native American, or Latino—to bear on the decisions they make, every vignette in the book encourages the class to voice women's and minorities' views and to deal with the diversity on two levels—the diversity present in our classrooms and the diversity that has characterized the United States throughout our history.

How *Key Decisions* is organized

The two volumes of *Key Decisions in U.S. History* are arranged chronologically, with decisions in American history from the fifteenth century to 1994. Each event is presented in the form of a vignette, some of which are paired around the same issue or event to provide an alternate perspective. To aid comprehension, many of the vignettes are supported by a visual organizer in the form of a timeline, map, or illustration. Each vignette is followed by comprehension questions based on the vignette and a series of solutions from which the students may choose. At the back of each volume, there is a separate Historical Notes section which presents teachers with vocabulary words that may need to be explained or visualized, additional information on each event, answers to the question "What really happened?", and sometimes teaching suggestions for the decision.

How to use *Key Decisions*

There are numerous ways to present and proceed through the vignettes. The paths to take depend on the kind of students in the class. For all students, the basic procedure is to read the vignette, make an individual decision about the best course of action, write out an explanation so that the reasoning is clear, discuss the decision with others in the group, and come to a group decision.

It is important that students truly understand the issues, so students first answer the comprehension questions either in class or as homework. We find it best for students to discuss answers in order to assure common understandings before proceeding to the actual decision.

Decision options are provided, but some teachers may want the students to think up their own

options. Depending on the class, the steps may be done wholly or in part as homework. The crux of the exercise—the discussion—must occur in class. We most often use the following procedure:

1. Prior to class, read the decision, the decision options, and the corresponding historical material. Note vocabulary and concepts with which students may have difficulty, and decide how to deal with them.

2. Set the scene. Briefly review what the class has been doing that leads up to the vignette/decision; pose a leading question; set the context. The timeline and/or pictures may help begin the discussion and deal with vocabulary.

3. The students read the vignette, silently or aloud.

4. To help them grasp the issues before making a decision, students answer the comprehension questions that focus on the vignette (main ideas, statements of fact vs. opinion,[*] inference, causes and effects, significant details, and sequences). The questions generally follow the sequence of the vignette and may be done as an oral or written activity, or skipped entirely at the teacher's discretion. We find it useful to discuss answers to these questions and ask our students to cite specific parts of the vignette to support their answers. As an overall comprehension check, we often ask students to predict what the decision question and some options might be.

5. Students read through the listed options and make their individual choices. Sometimes only one option is possible, but some decisions include several viable options. There is always an option for students to create their own alternate decision. Whatever option they choose, students should then thoroughly explain their reasoning in writing. This step provides the opportunity to refine and change their thinking prior to discussion.

6. Having made individual choices, students then meet in pairs, small groups, or as a whole class to discuss their decisions and reasons. They should be encouraged to listen carefully, to question, to disagree, to support, and to change their minds.

---

[*] Fact vs. opinion questions focus on whether statements are based on the speaker's opinion or are verifiable. Students should not confuse these statements with truth vs. falseness. Like opinions, factual statements can be true or false. For example, "The earth is flat" is a factual statement in that it can be checked and verified.

7. Students want to know "what really happened," so we usually tell them the historical decision, with reference to the choices they have just made. They can also be directed to the main history text or school library to investigate what really happened and report back to the class.

We are always finding new ways to use the "decisions" format. Most vignettes work well with students taking on different roles; others are particularly appropriate for group or class consensus. One student teacher used a press conference format in which half the class questioned the other half, who had taken on roles and made decisions accordingly.

Most vignettes stand on their own and require no previous knowledge of the historical event on which they are based. However, some decisions—those around the Civil War, for example—contain important information for the subsequent decision. Teachers following a chronologically based curriculum may sequence their use of decisions accordingly. The format is also appropriate for working with a theme-based syllabus. Themes like immigration, labor, and civil rights run throughout *Key Decisions*. A unit on voting rights could be built around decisions from the years 1620, 1682, 1777, 1848, 1866, 1887, 1905, 1920, 1964, and 1971. Another unit could examine Supreme Court decisions and issues of constitutionality.* Similarly, teachers may wish to focus on decisions dealing with Native Americans, African Americans, or women. The index is organized to help teachers working with either type of syllabus.

A note on visual organizers

The ability to understand visuals and their relation to written text is an important part of developing "history literacy." The wealth of visual information contained in history textbooks is of questionable value for students who are still developing these abilities. In *Key Decisions*, we have taken care to provide illustrations, photographs, maps, and timelines clearly related to individual vignettes. We envision these visual aids primarily as advance organizers to help students develop schema before reading the vignette. Illustrations and photographs give students a feeling for the people and events featured in the text. Maps and timelines locate the decision in space and time and, in some cases, show territorial changes or a progression of events described in the vignette. In most cases, the visuals support the vignette without suggesting the historical outcome, although some timelines connect several thematically related decisions.

Teachers can also use visuals to check student comprehension. After reading the vignette, students can be directed to locate any decision (or series of decisions) on a timeline or map, to draw their impressions of a historical event represented in a vignette, or even to locate corresponding images in the main history textbook or another history book.

The language of *Key Decisions*

The vignettes are written primarily at the fifth- to eighth-grade reading levels (Gunning Fogg Index and Flesch Index for Readability), in standard American English. Contractions and idiomatic expressions have been avoided in narratives but used where characters are speaking. In general, we have tried to provide a model for clear, organized, and formal writing. Treatment of vocabulary will differ depending on the students. Words we saw as potentially difficult for our ESL students are listed in the Historical Notes section for teachers to consider. Since so many words are used repeatedly, we find it useful to have students keep vocabulary notebooks. Students should be encouraged to demonstrate mastery of new words by using them in their responses to the comprehension questions and justification of their decision and/or by formal vocabulary quizzes.

Comprehension of many of the vignettes is often dependent on the pronoun reference, as indicated by many of the comprehension questions and their references to underlined words in the text. In the vignettes, we first address the student and provide an identity ("You are _____"). Thereafter, we have tried to use the first person (*I*,

---

* Originally, we asked students to decide if a decision was constitutional. Realizing that this requires knowledge they do not have, we have instead asked for their opinions: "What rights should English-speaking students have?" "Is segregation good for America?" "Should the U.S. permit segregation?" "Should women have the right to abortions?" This allows students to consider the underlying issues without extensive constitutional knowledge. We recommend that teachers take similar care when posing questions for discussion.

we, my, and so on) because we want the student to feel involved and active. However, in a few cases, the student is addressed as "you" throughout the vignette because it seems more realistic.

Titles (*Congressman* vs. *Congressperson* and names of ethnic groups (*Indians* vs. *Native Americans*) change over time. We have chosen to use the language and labels in use at the time of the decision. Thus, we refer to "Africans" in 1720, "black slaves" in 1831, "Negroes" in 1963, and "African Americans" in 1985. On issues of gender, we have tried to be as neutral as English allows, without denying historical fact. While "senator," "representative," and "legislator" work throughout, "congresswoman" was unrealistic before women's suffrage in 1920. In this matter, as with vocabulary, pronoun reference, and other types of comprehension questions, teachers should make adaptations to fit the needs of their students and their own beliefs.

We hope *Key Decisions in U.S. History* will encourage teachers and students to write their own decisions. We have included many important events and issues in U.S. history, but certainly there are others waiting to be turned into decisions/vignettes. A few examples are President Jackson deciding about the removal of the Cherokee, a decision to institute Social Security or Medicare, witnesses testifying about accused witches in Salem, voters deciding about a referendum on affirmative action, or the stock market crash. History is constantly "growing"—not only as new events occur and new issues arise, but also through the reexamination and new analyses of events and issues long past. In our classes, decisions have been an important tool in helping students feel the vitality of U.S. history and comprehend the main history text. We hope they work as well for you and your students.

President Lincoln

1861

How should we respond to the attack on Fort Sumter?

It is April 1861. Your are the new president, Abraham Lincoln.

After your inauguration last month, six southern states seceded from the Union. One state, South Carolina, seceded before you became president! These seven states have started a new country, the Confederate States of America. You think this is wrong. The Constitution does not give the states the right to leave the Union.

Now they are trying to take Fort Sumter in Charleston, South Carolina. Union soldiers there are surrounded by Confederate cannons. A few days ago, you ordered food and supplies to be sent to our soldiers inside the fort. Then the Confederates began to bomb it. First they attack our property and now our troops!

How should the U.S. government respond to this attack? When you became president, you promised to protect the United States. Should the North fight back? We have more factories, more workers, more railroads, more ships, and more money than the South, but we do not have a strong army that is ready to fight now. Many military leaders are from the South. They are leaving the U.S. military and joining the Confederacy. Some of your advisers say we should surrender Fort Sumter to the Confederates. If we fight back, more states might leave the Union. There might be a civil war between the North and the South.

Attack on Fort Sumter

Name _____ Date _____

President Lincoln: How should we respond to the attack
on Fort Sumter? *(continued)*

Comprehension

1. Who are you in this decision?

2. In paragraph 2, what do you think is wrong?

3. Why did the seven southern states start a new nation?

4. In paragraph 3, what does the word <u>they</u> refer to?

5. In paragraph 3, what does the word <u>it</u> refer to?

6. What is happening at Fort Sumter?

7. Why isn't the northern army ready to fight a war?

8. What is the best way to avoid this war?

9. If there is a war, which side will probably win? Why?

Decision

● *How should we respond to the attack on Fort Sumter? Choose one or more of the following options:*

 (a) Fight back now.

 (b) Order the U.S. military to prepare for war. We will fight back when our military forces are ready.

 (c) Don't fight back. Let the Confederates have Fort Sumter.

 (d) Don't fight back. Order the soldiers in the fort to wait as long as they can.

 (e) Do nothing.

 (f) Other: _____

● *Why did you decide that way? Plan how you will explain your decision to your classmates. Write out your reasoning completely.*

Name _____   Date _____

Northern States
They killed Lincoln! How should we punish the South?

It is April 15, 1865. You are an American in a northern state. Someone has just assassinated President Lincoln! Government soldiers have hunted down the murderer, John Wilkes Booth. He was part of a group of assassins. They also tried to kill Secretary of State William Seward, but he will probably live. Booth and his group hated Lincoln and the Union.

John Wilkes Booth

We Northerners are sad about the president's death. We were angry at the South for starting the war and killing so many of our soldiers, but now we are furious! Lincoln wanted to make peace with the South. He wanted to unite the states again quickly. Now Lincoln is dead. It is time to punish the South for what they have done to our country and to our president.

Abraham Lincoln

William Seward

Name _____ Date _____

Northern States: They killed Lincoln!
How should we punish the South? *(continued)*

Comprehension

1. Who are you in this decision?

2. Who tried to kill Seward?

3. Why are the northern states angry?

4. What part of the country do you think Booth is from?

5. What happened to William Seward?

6. What did Lincoln want to do after the war?

7. If he were alive, would Lincoln want to punish the South?

Decision

● *How should we punish the South? Choose one or more of the following options:*

(a) Raise federal taxes in the South.

(b) Make the southern states pay for the damages caused in the war.

(c) Make Southerners work for us as slaves.

(d) Abolish slavery.

(e) Keep our soldiers in the South.

(f) Make new laws that hurt the South. What should these laws say?

_____

(g) Don't let whites in the South vote.

(h) Give blacks the right to vote.

(i) The U.S. Congress should choose the new southern leaders.

(j) Take southern property.

(k) Give John Wilkes Booth and the other assassins a fair trial.

(l) Do not punish the South.

(m) Other: _____

● *Why did you decide that way? Plan how you will explain your decision to your classmates.*
  Write out your reasoning completely.

Republican Senator
How can we make southern states obey the Constitution?

It is 1866. You are a Republican senator from Massachusetts. Congress has just ratified two new amendments. The Thirteenth Amendment says that slavery is illegal in the United States. The Fourteenth Amendment makes whites and blacks equal. It gave citizenship to blacks and says the states have to treat them as citizens. But the southern states are passing new laws called "Black Codes" that discriminate against blacks. Under the Black Codes, blacks cannot vote, and they cannot speak in public. These laws also restrict when and how blacks can work.

The Emancipation Proclamation abolished slavery in the Confederate states three years ago, and now the Constitution says that slavery is illegal. But southern states are making a new kind of slavery for blacks. How can we guarantee their rights in the South? How can we make the Southern states obey the Constitution?

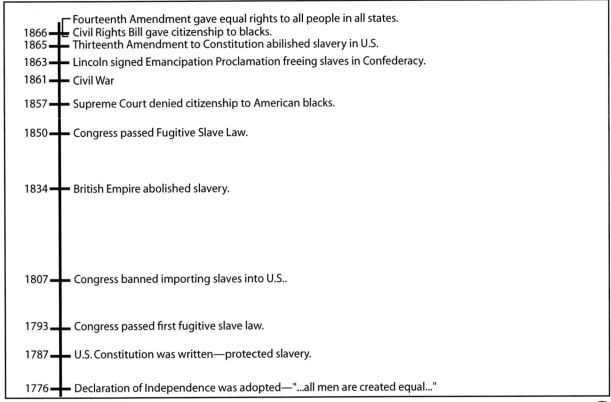

1866 ┬ Fourteenth Amendment gave equal rights to all people in all states.
     ├ Civil Rights Bill gave citizenship to blacks.
1865 ┼ Thirteenth Amendment to Constitution abilished slavery in U.S.
1863 ┼ Lincoln signed Emancipation Proclamation freeing slaves in Confederacy.
1861 ┼ Civil War
1857 ┼ Supreme Court denied citizenship to American blacks.
1850 ┼ Congress passed Fugitive Slave Law.
1834 ┼ British Empire abolished slavery.
1807 ┼ Congress banned importing slaves into U.S..
1793 ┼ Congress passed first fugitive slave law.
1787 ┼ U.S. Constitution was written—protected slavery.
1776 ┴ Declaration of Independence was adopted—"...all men are created equal..."

1866

Republican Senator: How can we make southern states obey the Constitution? *(continued)*

Comprehension

1. Who are you in this decision?

2. What do the new amendments say?

3. What are the Black Codes? What do they say?

4. Why are the southern states passing the Black Codes?

5. What do you want the southern states to do?

Decision

- *How can we make the Southern states obey the Thirteenth and Fourteenth Amendments? Choose as many options as you think are needed.*

    (a) Let the southern states decide if they will obey or not.

    (b) Amend the Constitution again to make the Black Codes illegal.

    (c) Attack the states that don't obey the Constitution.

    (d) Throw states with Black Codes out of the Union.

    (e) Make everyone who fought against the Union during the war promise to obey the Constitution.

    (f) Send federal soldiers to force these states to obey the Constitution.

    (g) Other: _____

- *Why did you decide that way? Plan how you will explain your decision to your classmates. Write out your reasoning completely.*

Lakota

Should we sign the Fort Laramie Treaty?

1868

It is November 1868. You belong to the Lakota nation—a large and powerful group of Native Americans who live on the northern Great Plains. You are now at Fort Laramie. The U.S. government has asked you to go there to make a peace treaty.

Many people agree with the great war chief Red Cloud. He says that the whites have broken all the treaties in the past. The whites keep trying to steal your hunting grounds. The whites say they only want to build a road for white people to use to go through your land. Red Cloud says the truth is that the white people come looking for gold. When they find it, they do not obey the treaty. The treaty says they will only pass through your land. But the white people don't pass through your land—they stop and build towns. More white people come looking for gold, and they stay. Now they are even building a railroad across the plains. This frightens the animals that you hunt. You try to stop the railroad, but the government sends soldiers. They build

forts and fight against your people. The soldiers attack your villages and kill your women, children, and old people. Red Cloud says he cannot trust white men's treaties.

Now they want you to sign another treaty. The treaty will give you complete control of a very big piece of land, the Great Sioux Reservation, west of the Missouri River. The treaty says no whites can cross the land without your permission. No whites can live on that land without your permission. No whites will ever bother your people on that land. The U.S. government will send gifts of clothes and supplies. It will send teachers, a doctor, a farmer, a carpenter, a blacksmith, and an engineer to teach and help your people.

In return, the whites want your people to stop fighting against the railroad they are now building. They want you to promise to let them build roads off the reservation. Also, they want you to promise never to attack any white people or their property.

Red Cloud

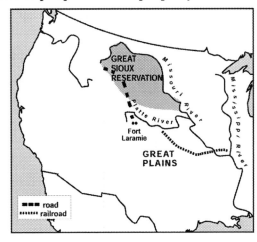

Lakota: Should we sign the Fort Laramie Treaty? *(continued)*

Comprehension

1. Who are you in this situation?

2. Why are you at Fort Laramie?

3. Why doesn't Red Cloud think the Lakota should sign the treaty?

4. What frightens the animals that you hunt?

5. Why don't the Lakota want the whites to build a railroad across the Great Plains?

6. What do the whites want you to agree to in this treaty?

7. What do the whites promise to give you in this treaty?

8. Who will control the Great Sioux Reservation if you sign the new treaty?

9. What do the whites want to do after you sign the treaty?

10. Do you have to sign the treaty?

11. What will happen if you don't sign the treaty?

12. What will happen if you sign the treaty?

13. What are reasons to sign the treaty?

14. What are reasons not to sign the treaty?

Decision

- *Should we sign the Fort Laramie treaty? Choose one or more of the following options:*

    (a) Sign the treaty. Maybe you can believe the whites this time. If they keep their promises, it will be good for your people.

    (b) Sign the treaty. If they break the treaty, you can make war on them again.

    (c) Do not sign this treaty. It is not a good treaty. You want the treaty to say

    _____

    (d) Never sign white men's treaties. They break the treaties and steal from you.

    (e) Attack the soldiers now. If you kill enough of them, maybe they will stop coming to your land.

    (f) Other: _____

- *Why did you decide that way? Plan how you will explain your decision to your classmates. Write out your reasoning completely.*

1870

Chinese Worker
Should you bring your family to America?

It is 1870. You are a Chinese man living in California. You came to the United States five years ago with many other men from China. You came to build a railroad because the Americans do not have enough workers. Your family stayed in China. Sometimes you get letters from them, but you haven't seen them in five years.

Building the railroad was hard and dangerous. Sometimes there were explosions and accidents. Many workers died. But now the railroad is finished. Now it is possible to take a train from New York to San Francisco, all the way across the United States.

What will you do next? Should you go back to China? Your wife's letters say that life in China is very difficult now. Some of the railroad workers have already returned to China. Others have decided to stay in America. The railroad is finished, but maybe they can find other jobs here. If you send money, your family can buy boat tickets and come to America.

Is the United States a good place for a Chinese family? There are more jobs in America than in China. Maybe you can live better here. But what about the people? Some Americans are friendly. However, many do not like Chinese people. They say that it was all right for foreigners to work on the railroad, but the railroad is complete now. These people say the Chinese workers should return to China. They say that America does not need them anymore.

Chinese railroad workers

© 1997 J. Weston Walch, Publisher   9   *Key Decisions in U.S. History, Vol. 2*

Name _____ Date _____

Comprehension

1. Who are you in this decision?

2. Whom did you receive letters from while you were working on the railroad?

3. Why are you in America?

4. In what year did you last see your family?

5. In paragraph 4, what does <u>these people</u> refer to?

6. Why do some people say that Chinese workers should return to China?

7. How do you know about the conditions in China now?

8. Which country has more jobs now—the U.S. or China?

9. Why don't you continue to work on the railroad?

10. If you want to bring your family to America, what do you need to do?

11. What is the decision you have to make?

Decision

● *What should you do? Choose one or more of the following options:*

    (a) Find a new job in California and stay in America.

    (b) Move to another state where railroads are still being built.

    (c) Leave America. Go back to your family in China.

    (d) Bring your family to the United States now.

    (e) Start a new family in America.

    (f) Other: _____

● *Why did you decide that way? Plan how you will explain your decision to your classmates. Write out your reasoning completely.*

1878

Southern Whites
How can we get our old way of life back?

It is 1878. You are a white state legislator from North Carolina. Before the Civil War, white people controlled black people in America. When the Confederacy lost the war, the government amended the Constitution to give new rights to blacks. The Thirteenth Amendment abolished slavery. The Fourteenth Amendment gave blacks citizenship and said the states had to treat them as citizens. The Fifteenth Amendment said blacks could vote.

Now blacks own land and businesses. They vote and hold public offices. White and black people use the same schools, churches, restaurants, and parks. We don't want to share these things with black people! We don't want black people to be equal to white people.

The national government knows we are unhappy. It sent soldiers to force the southern state governments to obey the new amendments. The federal soldiers occupied the South for almost 10 years. The northern soldiers made southern leaders swear to be loyal to the United States. They even stopped some of our best leaders from running for public office, just because they used to be in the Confederate government! In their place, we have black politicians and these local scalawags who are cooperating with the federal government. The worst people are the carpetbaggers down from the North. They say they are here to help the South, but we think they are using our state governments to get rich. If they really want to help, they should go back home and leave us alone!

Since the war, the Republican party has won every presidential election. The Republicans still control both the Senate and the House of Representatives, but most of the southern state governments are Democratic. We don't agree with Republican ideas.

The new president, Rutherford B. Hayes, ordered all the federal soldiers to leave the southern states last year. Now they are gone. There is no one here to tell us what to do.

President Rutherford B. Hayes

Name _____   Date _____

  Southern Whites: How can we get our old way of life back? *(continued)*

Comprehension

1. Who are you in this decision?

2. Which amendment gives black people the rights of citizens?

3. In paragraph 2, what does the word <u>We</u> refer to?

4. In paragraph 3, what does the word <u>they</u> refer to?

5. Why were the federal soldiers in the South?

6. Who are the new state leaders in the southern state governments?

7. For each statement, write *F* for fact or *O* for opinion. Remember that facts are things that can be checked and agreed to by everyone. Opinions are a person's own ideas.

   (a) The new amendments are bad for the South.

   (b) Blacks now have more power than they did before the war.

   (c) The northern carpetbaggers are here to steal our money.

   (d) The federal soldiers left because the president told them to.

   (e) Southern whites have lost some of their power.

   (f) Most of the southern state governments are Republican.

Decision

- *How can we get our old way of life back? Choose one or more of the following options:*

   (a) We should obey the new amendments to the Constitution.

   (b) We should ignore the new amendments.

   (c) We should try to amend the Constitution again to make it say what we want.

   (d) We should separate from the Union again.

   (e) We should pass new state laws to give whites more power than blacks.

   (f) Other: _____

- *Why did you decide that way? Plan how you will explain your decision to your classmates. Write out your reasoning completely.*

U.S. Congress
1879
Should we restrict Chinese immigration?

It is 1879. You are a member of Congress. People from all over the world are leaving their countries and coming to live in the United States. In the western states, most of the new immigrants are Chinese. At first, they came to look for gold in California. Later, the federal government signed a treaty with China, because the western states needed Chinese workers to build the railroads. The treaty said that Chinese people could work in the United States, but they could not become American citizens. Now there are more than 100,000 Chinese immigrants living in our country. <u>They</u> are 10 percent of the population of California!

Many people are complaining that there are too many Chinese immigrants. There is no more gold to mine, and the railroads are finished, too. There are not enough jobs for everyone. The labor unions complain that Chinese workers do not join the unions. They work long hours for low pay. <u>This</u> takes jobs away from American workers.

The Chinese workers are different from the European immigrants who came here before. The Europeans who came to the United States stayed here. Their children and their grandchildren became Americans. But many Chinese work for a while, then take their savings and return to China. They do not try to become Americans. Some people say that the Chinese should not be in America because they are so different from the American people. <u>Their</u> food, their language, and their customs are different. They even look different. Some western cities are making special laws limiting where Chinese people can work and go to school. White workers have attacked Chinese workers and businesses in Colorado, California, and Washington.

Should the government restrict Chinese immigration? Some people and groups say the U.S. should stop some or all of the Chinese from coming here. We should break the old treaty. However, China is an important trading partner for American businesses. If we break our treaty, the Chinese government might stop us from doing business in China.

White men attacking Chinese workers, late 1800's

U.S. Congress: Should we restrict Chinese immigration? *(continued)*

Comprehension

1. Who are you in this decision?

2. In paragraph 1, what does the word <u>They</u> refer to?

3. Why did the United States want Chinese workers to come to the U.S.?

4. Can Chinese workers become U.S. citizens?

5. What happened first—the California Gold Rush or the U.S. treaty with China?

6. In paragraph 2, what does <u>This</u> refer to?

7. Why are American workers angry about Chinese immigration?

8. In paragraph 3, what does the word <u>Their</u> refer to?

9. Who came to the U.S. first—the Europeans or the Chinese? Do you think that is important?

10. How are the Chinese workers different from European immigrants?

11. What might happen if America breaks the treaty with China?

12. What do you think the question to decide about will be?

Decision

● *Should we restrict Chinese immigration? Choose one or more of the following options:*

(a) No, let the Chinese come to America like immigrants from other countries.

(b) Not yet. Wait until the treaty with China expires.

(c) Yes. Let's restrict Chinese immigration now. How many Chinese people can come into the U.S. each year? _____. What kind of people should these immigrants be—men, women, children, or laborers? _____

(d) Yes. Let's stop Chinese immigration completely now.

(e) Other: _____

● *Why did you decide that way? Plan how you will explain your decision to your classmates. Write out your reasoning completely.*

American Citizens
Should we protect our forests?

It is 1891. You are an American citizen. Congress is discussing the Forest Reserve Act. If Congress passes this bill, it will let the president set aside public forest lands. The government would be able to protect forests and all the water, minerals, and animals that are in <u>them</u>.

Conservationists like the act. They say the government has given away too much land. Mining companies, railroads, and timber companies have been cutting down the forests. Already, 75 percent of America's first forests have been cut down. Soon there will be no more forests. Wildlife will have no place to live. Water is becoming polluted. Conservationists say that the government must protect our natural resources.

Many powerful companies do not like the act. They say that America must use its natural resources. We need wood and the valuable minerals to build houses and railroads. We need to mine coal to make steel. America will stop being powerful if we do not use our natural resources. People will lose jobs. The government has already reserved Yellowstone in Wyoming and Yosemite Valley in California for protection. <u>These</u> are some of the best forests we have! How many forests will the government reserve? Our industries need these trees and minerals. We must not spend one penny on scenery!

Yosemite National Park

American Citizens: Should we protect our forests? *(continued)*

Comprehension

1. Who are you in this story?

2. What does the word <u>them</u> refer to in the first paragraph?

3. Who likes the Forest Reserve Act?

4. Why do they like it?

5. Who opposes the Forest Reserve Act?

6. Why do they oppose it?

7. What does the word <u>These</u> refer to in the third paragraph?

8. According to the conservationists, what will happen to America if the Forest Reserve Act passes?

9. According to the companies, what will happen to America if the Forest Reserve Act passes?

Decision

- *Should Congress pass the Forest Reserve Act? Choose one of the following options:*

    (a) Congress should pass the Forest Reserve Act.

    (b) Congress should not pass the Forest Reserve Act.

    (c) Other: _____

- *Why did you decide that way? Plan how you will explain your decision to your classmates. Write out your reasoning completely.*

Ida Wells

How can we stop the lynchings?

1892

It is 1892. You are Ida Wells, a black woman and owner of a newspaper, *The Free Press*, in Memphis, Tennessee. In Memphis and other southern cities, white mobs are killing black people. When these people are angry at a black person, <u>they</u> do not use the law. Instead, they kidnap the person. Sometimes, they just scare the person, but sometimes they torture and even kill <u>him</u>. This is called lynching. In the last 10 years, white mobs have killed hundreds of black people! In Memphis last week, a group of whites killed three black store owners. How can we stop these mobs from killing more black people?

Some people say that the best way for blacks to stop the lynching is to force the town to protect black citizens. A boycott would make the town government pay attention to this problem. Memphis depends on black workers and black consumers. What could we boycott? Perhaps we could stop buying from white-owned businesses, stop riding the city streetcar system, and stop working for white people.

Other people say that whites in Memphis will never listen to blacks. Maybe the federal government could help us stop the lynching.

Some blacks say that we need guns. In Memphis, white people can own guns, but blacks cannot. If we had guns, we could

Ida Wells

defend ourselves against the white mobs. Or we could attack white people before they attack <u>us</u>.

Your newspaper is important in Memphis. Whatever you write in *The Free Press* could convince black people here what to do. It could also get you into trouble. The white mobs could try to shut down the newspaper, or even attack you if they do not like what you write.

Ida Wells: How can we stop the lynchings? *(continued)*

Comprehension

1. Who are you in this decision?

2. In paragraph 1, what does the word <u>they</u> refer to?

3. In paragraph 1, what does the word <u>him</u> refer to?

4. How could a boycott help blacks in Memphis?

5. What are some things blacks could boycott?

6. In paragraph 4, what does the word <u>us</u> refer to?

7. Why doesn't Memphis protect blacks?

8. Why don't blacks buy guns to protect themselves?

9. How can a newspaper help solve the problem of lynching?

Decision

● *What will you write in your newspaper? Choose one or more options:*

   (a) Blacks should get guns and attack the whites.

   (b) Blacks should get guns and defend themselves when the whites attack them.

   (c) Blacks should stop shopping in white-owned stores.

   (d) Blacks should boycott the city streetcar system.

   (e) Blacks should leave Memphis and go somewhere safer. Where? _____

   (f) Blacks should be more careful not to bother whites in Memphis.

   (g) The federal government should send soldiers to Memphis to protect blacks.

   (h) Don't write anything in the newspaper.

   (i) Other: _____

● *Why did you decide that way? Plan how you will explain your decision to your classmates. Write out your reasoning completely.*

© 1997 J. Weston Walch, Publisher

Supreme Court
Should the U.S. permit segregation?

It is 1896. You are a justice of the Supreme Court. The Court is deciding if segregation is constitutional in the United States. Here is the case: the state of Louisiana has a law that says blacks and whites cannot sit together on trains. The law says that railroad companies must have some cars for blacks and <u>others</u> for whites.

A colored man named Homer Plessy was arrested for sitting in the white section of the train. He says that he is not guilty because the Louisiana law is wrong. He says that the Thirteenth and Fourteenth Amendments to the Constitution make segregation illegal in all the United States.

Judge Ferguson of Louisiana says segregation is legal when there are "separate but equal" trains. If the railroad companies have cars for blacks that are as good as the <u>ones</u> for whites, then <u>they</u> are not going against the Constitution.

This case is not just about trains. There are segregation laws all over the United States—in schools, theaters, restaurants, and hotels. Some states even have laws that say a black person cannot marry a white person! If the Supreme Court decides Ferguson is right, then local and state governments can continue to make segregation laws. If we decide that Plessy is right, the federal government will not permit segregation anywhere in the U.S. That would be a big change for many parts of our country, especially the southern states.

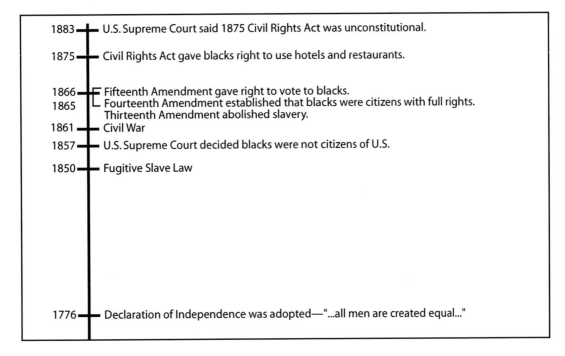

1883 — U.S. Supreme Court said 1875 Civil Rights Act was unconstitutional.

1875 — Civil Rights Act gave blacks right to use hotels and restaurants.

1866 — Fifteenth Amendment gave right to vote to blacks.
1865 — Fourteenth Amendment established that blacks were citizens with full rights.
Thirteenth Amendment abolished slavery.
1861 — Civil War
1857 — U.S. Supreme Court decided blacks were not citizens of U.S.

1850 — Fugitive Slave Law

1776 — Declaration of Independence was adopted—"...all men are created equal..."

1896   ## Supreme Court: Should the U.S. permit segregation? *(continued)*

Comprehension

1. Who are you in this decision?

2. In paragraph 1, what does the word <u>others</u> refer to?

3. What do the Thirteenth and Fourteenth Amendments to the Constitution say?

4. Who wants segregation to end—Plessy or Ferguson?

5. Why is the Louisiana law called "separate but equal"?

6. In paragraph 3, what does the word <u>ones</u> refer to?

7. In paragraph 3, what does the word <u>they</u> refer to?

8. What things are segregated in our country?

9. What part of the U.S. will change the most if the Supreme Court ends segregation?

Decision

● *Should the United States permit segregation? Choose one of the following options:*

(a) No.

(b) Yes. States have the right to make any segregation laws they want to.

(c) Yes. However, states can only have segregation laws that do not conflict with the Thirteenth and Fourteenth Amendments to the Constitution.

(d) Other: _____

● *Why did you decide that way? Plan how you will explain your decision to your classmates. Write out your reasoning completely.*

President Cleveland

Should we make immigrants pass a literacy test?

1896

It is December 1896. You are U.S. President Grover Cleveland. In a few days, your term of office will end, and William McKinley will become the new president. While you are still president, there is an

Grover Cleveland

important decision to make. Congress has just passed a bill which says that new immigrants to the U.S. must pass a literacy test. If the immigrants cannot read in English or another language, they cannot stay in our country. Many new immigrants cannot read. They will fail the test. As president, you must sign the bill or veto it. You could leave the decision to the new president, but McKinley will probably sign the bill.

What do other Americans think about the literacy test bill?

LABOR UNIONS: There are not enough jobs for Americans. When immigrants come here, they take jobs away from American workers. Immigrants are bad for our labor unions. They work for very low wages and sometimes they are strikebreakers. For American workers, the fewer immigrants, the better!

BUSINESS OWNERS: Immigrants are good for American business. They work hard, and we can pay them less than we pay American workers. Without immigrants, maybe we will not have enough workers. Besides, most of the jobs we have for immigrants are physical labor jobs. It does not matter if immigrants

can read. To work for us, they need their muscles, not their brains.

IMMIGRANTS ALREADY IN THE U.S.: Except for the Indians, we are all immigrants. America is a great country because people from all over the world come here to live and work. Some people have an education when they come to America, but many do not. Some immigrants do not have the chance to go to school in their own countries. But the United States is the land of opportunity. There is enough here for everyone.

WHITE SUPREMACIST GROUPS: It is true that many Americans come from immigrant families. But the English, Irish, German, Scandinavian, and French groups that came in the past were white. Except for the Irish and French, most of them were Protestants. Now the immigrants coming to our country are different. They are from Asia and Central Europe. Most of them are poor and uneducated, too. They are not white, and many of them are Catholic, Jewish, and Buddhist. These people are not as good as white, Protestant people. If we let them into the United States, they will mix with whites. Our country will become weak.

POLITICAL PARTIES: Immigrants cannot vote in most elections until they become U.S. citizens. But when they become citizens, there will be millions of new voters. That is enough votes to win local, state, and national elections. If our political party is good to the immigrants now, they will vote for our party in the future.

1896

President Cleveland: Should we make immigrants pass a literacy test? *(continued)*

Comprehension

1. Who are you in this decision?

2. In paragraph 3, what does the word <u>They</u> refer to?

3. Who were Protestants and who were not?

4. In paragraph 6, what do the words <u>These people</u> refer to?

5. What groups want the president to sign the literacy bill?

6. What groups are against the literacy bill?

7. Can immigrants vote in U.S. elections?

8. Why does President Cleveland have to decide now?

9. For each statement, write *F* for fact or *O* for opinion. Remember that facts are things that can be checked and agreed to by everyone. Opinions are a person's own ideas.

   (a) Immigrants should be literate.
   (b) Now the immigrants are different than in the past.
   (c) Most of the new immigrants are poor and uneducated.
   (d) They are not as good as white Protestants.
   (e) To work for us, they need their muscles, not their brains.

Decision

● *Should we make immigrants pass a literacy test? Choose one or more of the following options:*

   (a) Yes. All new immigrants 21 years and older must pass a reading test in English.
   (b) Yes. All new immigrants must pass a reading test, but it can be in any language.
   (c) We should give immigrants a period of _____ years to pass a reading test. If they cannot pass the test in this time, they will have to leave the U.S.
   (d) No. We should not force immigrants to pass a reading test.
   (e) Other: _____

● *Why did you decide that way? Plan how you will explain your decision to your classmates. Write out your reasoning completely.*

U.S. Congress

Should the U.S. go to war against Spain?

1898

It is 1898. You are a member of Congress. The *Maine*, an American battleship, has exploded near Havana, Cuba. More than 250 American sailors died in this explosion. President McKinley thinks that the Spanish government is responsible. He is asking Congress to declare war on Spain. We have been close to war for months because of the Spanish government's actions in Cuba. Will you vote to declare war now? Before you vote, listen to what Americans are saying.

THE PRESS: The American people are ready for war against Spain. The Cuban people have been fighting a revolution against Spain for three years. The Spanish army has 50,000 soldiers. They are killing Cuban citizens as if <u>they</u> were flies. This war is like the American Revolution—a small country fighting for freedom from a powerful European empire. Cuba should be a free and independent nation, and the U.S. should help Cubans get their independence. Now Spain has blown up an American navy ship. Congress should declare war immediately.

BUSINESS LEADERS: U.S. trade in Cuba is growing quickly. Last year it was nearly $30 million. We will make even more money if there is peace. If we declare war on Spain, our plantations in Cuba could be damaged. If there is war, we will lose money. Besides, we do not know if the Cuban government would want U.S. business there. But we know Spain

likes to do business with us. We should negotiate peace with Spain. That is the safe thing to do.

OTHER BUSINESS LEADERS: There is already a war in Cuba! The Spanish government is too weak to defeat the rebels. We are losing money now because of the war. We should support the Cubans because they are going to win eventually. Of course the new Cuban leaders will do business with us. They need our dollars. And if we help them, they will be our friends. Declare war against Spain now.

THEODORE ROOSEVELT: This war is not about only Cuba. This island is important for us, but it is only one small piece of land. The United States produces more than we can consume at home. We need to export our products to foreign markets. Look at the Spanish Empire. It includes Cuba, Puerto Rico, the Philippines, and other islands in the Pacific. If we defeat Spain, all those territories will be ours. We can sell our products to the people who live <u>there</u>. We can help spread democracy, too. If we control these lands, we will have ports and military bases closer to China and Japan. If we beat Spain, we will become one of the most powerful nations in the world.

President McKinley says he did not want to fight a war with Spain, but now he believes war is necessary.

U.S. Congress: Should the U.S. go to war against Spain? *(continued)*

Comprehension

1. Who are you in this decision?

2. In paragraph 2, what does the word <u>they</u> refer to?

3. Which group(s) want to declare war on Spain? What are their reasons?

4. In paragraph 5, what does the word <u>there</u> refer to?

5. Which groups oppose war with Spain? What are their reasons?

6. What do business leaders disagree about? Why do they disagree?

7. Why is it important to sell American products in other countries?

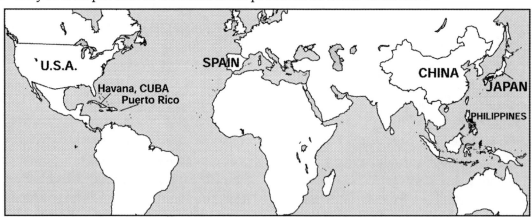

Decision

- *Should the United States go to war against Spain? Choose one or more of the following options:*

  (a) Yes, but if we defeat Spain, we should not take her territories.
  (b) Yes, and if we defeat Spain, we will take all her territories.
  (c) No. We should not go to war against Spain.
  (d) We should not send American soldiers, but we should give money and guns to the Cuban soldiers.
  (e) We should negotiate with the Spanish more before we make this decision.
  (f) Other: _____

- *Why did you decide that way? Plan how you will explain your decision to your classmates. Write out your reasoning completely.*

U.S. Congress
1899
Should we control the Philippine Islands?

It is 1899. You are a senator in the U.S. Congress. The war against Spain is over. In only four months, American soldiers have defeated Spain. Now the United States controls the Spanish Empire. We have Cuba and Puerto Rico in the Atlantic, and we have Guam and the Philippine Islands in the Pacific. President McKinley wants us to ratify the peace treaty with Spain. The Treaty of Paris says that the U.S. will pay Spain $20 million, and then Puerto Rico, Guam, and the Philippines will become U.S. territories.

The Philippines is the biggest and most important part of the treaty. There are 7,000 islands in this colony, and they have important minerals such as coal and gold. The land is excellent for growing crops such as coffee and tea, which we cannot grow in the United States. These islands are close to Japan and China, too. They would make a good place for American ships to stop on their way to Asia. We could even have navy bases there. Many people in America want to keep the Philippines. These islands will be excellent for the United States militarily and economically.

There's just one problem. The Filipinos do not want to be part of the United States. They want the Philippines to be an independent nation. They welcomed our help against Spain for independence. Now that the war is over, however, the Filipinos have written a new constitution. They do not want a new foreign country to rule them. They want freedom, just as we did in our revolution.

Many Americans agree with the Filipinos. They say that the United States is a great country because her people believe in freedom. How can we take freedom away from the Filipino people? Are freedom and self-government only for Americans? If we pass this treaty, thousands of Filipino rebels will fight against the United States. Our army and navy are much stronger than the Filipinos' army. We can crush their soldiers easily, but then we will just be like the Spanish. This treaty is bad for the Philippines and bad for America, too.

President McKinley says the Filipinos are not ready for freedom and self-government yet. He says they are not as smart as Americans, so the United States must show them how to make a good government. He wants American missionaries to go to the Philippines and teach people about the Christian religion. American companies can teach Filipino workers how to work. McKinley says that someday, when the Filipinos are educated, they can have independence. Besides, if we do not take the Philippines, then another strong country will.

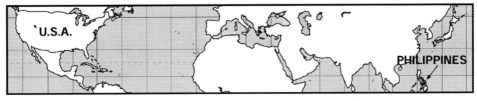

U.S. Congress: Should we control the Philippine Islands? *(continued)*

Comprehension

1. Who are you in this decision?

2. How does President McKinley want you to vote?

3. In paragraph 2, what do the words this colony refer to?

4. In paragraph 2, what does the word They refer to?

5. In paragraph 3, what does the word our refer to?

6. Who were the Filipinos fighting before the Americans?

7. Why are the Philippines good for U.S. trade with Asia?

8. In paragraph 4, what do the words this treaty refer to?

9. In paragraph 5, what does the word them refer to?

10. What other strong country might control the Philippines if we don't?

11. For each statement, write *F* for fact and O for opinion. Remember that facts are things that can be checked. Opinions are a person's own ideas.

    (a) The Filipinos are not ready for self-government yet.
    (b) The U.S. has gotten more territory because of the Spanish-American war.
    (c) Freedom and self-government are only for Americans.
    (d) The Filipinos have written a new constitution.
    (e) The U.S. is a great country because her people believe in freedom.

Decision

● *Should we ratify the Treaty of Paris? Choose one of the following options:*

    (a) Yes
    (b) No
    (c) Other: _____

● *Why did you decide that way? Plan how you will explain your decision to your classmates. Write out your reasoning completely.*

1905

Blacks
What is the best way for us to get social equality?

It is 1905. You are a black college student in Atlanta, Georgia.

In the United States, black people still don't have the same rights white people have. The Constitution says <u>we</u> do, but many states just ignore the Fourteenth and Fifteenth Amendments. In many places, we cannot own land or vote. We still have the worst jobs and the worst schools. There is a lot of violence against us, too. Last year, more than one hundred black people were killed by white groups such as the Ku Klux Klan.

How can we stop this racism? How can we force the states to obey the Constitution? There are two famous black leaders with very different ideas about how to solve the problem: Booker T. Washington and W.E.B. Du Bois.

Washington is the founder of Tuskegee Institute, a technical college for black Americans. He says that we have to be patient. The best way to get our rights is to work hard as farmers, carpenters, and tradespeople. If we work hard at these jobs, white people will see that we are good and responsible people. Then <u>they</u> will stop discriminating against us. If we demand civil rights now, there will be more violence against us. We must be patient.

Du Bois is a college professor. He believes we should not *wait* for social equality. If we want whites to treat us as equals, we have to study and become doctors, lawyers, and teachers. Black Americans should demand the civil rights that the Constitution guarantees to all Americans. But we have to act now. If we are patient, we will never get these rights.

Booker T. Washington

W.E.B. Dubois

Blacks: What is the best way for us to get social equality? *(continued)*

Comprehension

1. Who are you in this decision?

2. In paragraph 2, what does the word <u>we</u> refer to?

3. In paragraph 4, what does the word <u>they</u> refer to?

4. How are Washington and Du Bois the same?

5. In what ways are Washington and Du Bois different?

Decision

● *Who do you think is right—Washington or Du Bois? Choose one of the following options:*

   (a) Washington

   (b) Du Bois

   (c) Neither one is right. To get our rights, we should _____

   _____

   (d) Other: _____

● *Why did you decide that way? Plan how you will explain your decision to your classmates. Write out your reasoning completely.*

Native Americans
Should we send our children to white people's schools?

It is 1908. You are an Ojibway Indian living near Lake Michigan. Our people have lived in this place for many years. When the whites came, our lives changed. We still farm and hunt and fish, but life is more difficult now. The whites took a lot of our land. There are too many people around now. The hunting and fishing are not as good as they used to be. Many people still live the old ways, but others are learning the ways of the whites.

The world is changing. How should we teach our children? Some people say that Ojibway children should go to white people's schools. Then they can learn to speak and write the whites' language. They will be able to have jobs like the whites and help us understand their laws.

But some people say that white people's schools will change our young people too much. They will become whites and forget our Ojibway language and religion. If our children go to white people's schools, they won't be Ojibway anymore. These people say that we should keep the old Ojibway ways.

Ojibway children in school

Native Americans: Should we send our children to white people's schools? *(continued)*

Comprehension

1. Who are you in this decision?

2. What used to be better for us?

3. In paragraph 1, what does the word <u>others</u> refer to?

4. In paragraph 2, what does the word <u>they</u> refer to?

5. Whose laws will our children learn about?

6. Why do some people want to send Ojibway children to white people's schools?

7. Why do some people oppose sending Ojibway children to white people's schools?

8. Do the Ojibway and the whites have the same language?

9. What language do the whites have?

10. How is life different for the Ojibway people now?

Decision

● *Should we send our children to white people's schools?*

    (a) No. Ojibway students should not attend white schools.

    (b) Yes. All Ojibway students should attend white schools.

    (c) Allow the family of each child to decide.

    (d) Allow each child to decide.

    (e) Establish Ojibway schools for our children.

    (f) Other: _____

● *Why did you decide that way? Plan how you will explain your decision to your classmates. Write out your reasoning completely.*

American Citizens
Should we get involved in the war in Europe?

It is 1917. You are an American citizen. There is another war in Europe. This war is different from earlier wars. In the past, most countries used their armies to protect their own borders. Now, most European countries have treaties to protect themselves and their allies from attack. In this war, the Allies—Britain, France, Italy, and Russia—are on one side. The Central Powers—Germany, Austria-Hungary, and Japan—are on the other side. The fighting began when an assassin killed an Austrian leader. Now almost all the European nations are fighting. The armies have many soldiers and modern weapons. Thousands of people are dying in Europe.

The United States did not sign these treaties. We are trying to stay neutral, although we are friendly with the governments of the Allies. We have been selling guns and other supplies to the British military. This is great business for our merchants, but Germany and the other Central Powers do not think America should be helping Britain. The Germans say that they will attack any ships carrying weapons to their enemies. Two years ago, a German submarine attacked and sank a British ship called the *Lusitania*. It was a British ship, but more than 120 American passengers died. The ship was carrying American guns and ammunition to England. Though some people disagreed with him, President Wilson still wanted the U.S. to be neutral in the war. He said that it was a European war and that America should not get involved.

Recently, the Germans have begun to attack American ships. Now Wilson wants the U.S. to join the Allies and fight against the Central Powers. He wants one million American men to volunteer. If we join the fighting, many of those men will die.

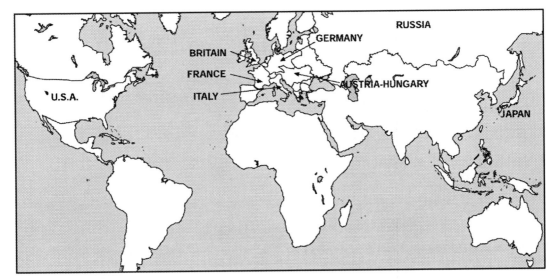

Name _____ Date _____

 1917 | **American Citizens: Should we get involved in the war in Europe?**
(continued)

Comprehension

1. Who are you in this story?

2. What is different about this war?

3. What are the names of the two sides fighting this war?

4. Are we helping any countries in this war?

5. In paragraph 2, what does the word <u>their</u> refer to?

6. Why did President Wilson change his mind about the war?

7. Why do you care about the sinking of the *Lusitania*?

8. If we join this war, who will be our allies?

9. If we join this war, who will be our enemies?

10. How many volunteers does President Wilson want?

Decision

● *What should we do about the war in Europe? Choose one or more of the following options:*

   (a) Don't join the war.

   (b) Join the war.

   (c) Ask the Germans to pay for the American lives and property
        lost aboard the *Lusitania*.

   (d) Continue selling arms to England and the Allies.

   (e) Lend money to the Allies to keep fighting.

   (f) Build up the U.S. military to prepare for war.

   (g) Sell arms to any country that pays us.

   (h) Stay neutral.

   (i) Other: _____

● *Why did you decide that way? Plan how you will explain your decision to your classmates.
   Write out your reasoning completely.*

Name _____   Date _____

U.S. Congress
Should America join the League of Nations?

It is 1919. You are a senator in the U.S. Congress. The Great War in Europe has just ended. More than 115,000 American soldiers died in this terrible war. How can we stop <u>this</u> from happening again?

Last year, President Wilson made a treaty with European leaders to form a "League of Nations." The League is a way for countries to discuss their problems together instead of fighting. The president says America should join the League of Nations so that our soldiers will never have to fight a foreign war again. He wants Congress to approve his plan for the League of Nations. If Congress doesn't approve the treaty, the U.S. cannot join.

Some senators oppose the treaty. They say that the Great War was caused by too many alliances among the European countries. They are worried that the League of Nations would be a world government with the power to tell our national government what to do. What if the League of Nations said that the United States had to send soldiers to Europe again? Our Constitution says that only Congress can declare war. If we join the League of Nations, will Congress lose this power? Massachusetts senator Henry Cabot Lodge says that he will vote against the League, unless only Congress can still decide which wars America will fight.

1914	World War I
1912	Balkan Wars
1911	Italo-Turkish War
1904	Russo-Japanese War
1899	Boer War.
1898	Spanish American War
1895	Ethiopian War
1879	War of the Pacific (Chile, Bolivia, Peru).
1870	Franco-Prussian War
1866	Seven Weeks' War (Prussia-Austria)
1861	U.S. Civil War
1853	Crimean War
1846	Siberian Wars / Mexican War
1812	War of 1812
1803	Napoleonic Wars

President Woodrow Wilson

1919   U.S. Congress: Should America join the League of Nations? *(continued)*

Comprehension

1. Who are you in this decision?

2. In paragraph 1, what does the word <u>this</u> refer to?

3. Why is the League of Nations important?

4. Who is in favor of the League? Why?

5. Who opposes the League? Why?

6. For each statement, write *T* for true or *F* for false:

   (a) The Great War was fought in the United States.

   (b) President Wilson can approve this treaty even if the Senate votes against it.

   (c) Now only Congress can decide if America will fight a war.

Decision

- *Should America join the League of Nations? Choose one of the following options:*

   (a) Yes. We should vote for the president's plan.

   (b) Yes, but only if the president agrees to change the treaty. What changes do you want to make before you will sign?

   _____

   (c) No. America should not join the League of Nations.

   (d) Other: _____

- *Why did you decide that way? Plan how you will explain your decision to your classmates. Write out your reasoning completely.*

1920 Negroes in the South
Should we move north?

It is 1920. We are Negroes living in Louisiana. This is a poor state and life is hard for us here. Louisiana schools are segregated, and most schools for blacks are not as good as white schools. There are special state laws to stop Negroes from voting, traveling, and owning property in Louisiana.

Most of us are farmers, but we do not own the land we work on. Whites own the land, and they rent it to us. The rent contract says we have to buy everything from the landlord's store. The prices are so high that it is almost impossible to save money. Many people owe money to their landlord. If we move to a new place, the new landlord can collect our old debts.

People are talking about life in the northern cities. They say that the schools are better in the North. Negroes can vote and own property there, too. And there are more jobs in the North. In Detroit, Cleveland, Chicago, and other cities, the factories need workers.

It would be hard for us to move north. Train tickets are expensive, and we will have to find a new place to live. Most of us are farmers. Can we learn to work in a factory? What will it be like to live in a city? We don't know many people in the North. Will we make new friends? Will we be able to survive in the North?

Sharecroppers in the South

1920

Negroes in the South: Should we move north? *(continued)*

Comprehension

1. Who are we in this decision?

2. What kind of job do most Negroes in the South have?

3. Who owns the land where most Negro farmers work?

4. What kind of jobs are there in the North?

5. Why do we buy our goods in the landlord's store?

6. How would life be different for us in the North?

Decision

● *Should we leave Louisiana and move north? Choose one or more of the following options:*

  (a) No. It is better to stay here in Louisiana.

  (b) Yes. The family should move north as soon as possible.

  (c) Let's leave Louisiana and go to another southern state.

  (d) We should send some of the family north now to see what it is like there.

  (e) Other: _____

● *Why did you decide that way? Plan how you will explain your decision to your classmates. Write out your reasoning completely.*

Name _____   Date _____

State Legislators
Should women have the right to vote?

It is 1920. You are a state legislator. Should our state vote to amend the Constitution to allow women to vote? If 36 states ratify the amendment, all adult women will have the right to vote in all elections. Women have demanded this right for more than 70 years, and they have always been active in politics. Women were very important in the Revolutionary and Civil Wars. Women were important in the abolition and prohibition movements, and President Wilson says <u>we</u> would have lost the World War if women had not worked in this country while the men were fighting overseas.

Some people say that women should not have the right to vote. <u>They</u> believe that a woman's place is in the home, taking care of her family. If women can vote, they will want to run for public office. They will be too busy to take care of their homes, children, and husbands.

Other people say that women should have the right to vote. Women can already vote in some countries and in 15 U.S. states, including New York, Michigan, and most of the western states, women can vote in local and state elections only. <u>These people</u> ask, "Is America a democracy if only half of its citizens can vote?"

Women demanding the right to vote

State Legislators: Should women have the right to vote? *(continued)*

Comprehension

1. Who are you in this decision?

2. What do the women in the picture want?

3. What work do you think women did during the war?

4. In paragraph 1, what does the word <u>we</u> refer to?

5. In paragraph 2, what does the word <u>They</u> refer to?

6. In paragraph 3, what do the words <u>These people</u> refer to?

7. Can women vote anywhere in the U.S. in 1920? Where?

8. What can't women vote for?

Decision

● *Should we ratify the Nineteenth Amendment? Choose one of the following options:*

   (a) Yes, but only for some women. Which women should have the right to vote?

     _____

   (b) Yes. We should give all women 21 years and older the right to vote.

   (c) No. We should not ratify this amendment, but it is okay if the states let women vote in local and state elections.

   (d) No. We should not ratify this amendment. We should not permit women to vote in any elections anywhere in the U.S.

   (e) Other: _____

● *Why did you decide that way? Plan how you will explain your decision to your classmates. Write out your reasoning completely.*

President Roosevelt

1935

What should the government do to help poor people during the Depression?

Soup kitchen

It is 1935. You are President Franklin Roosevelt. When the American people elected you in 1932, the country was in a terrible depression. Many businesses and banks failed, and millions of Americans lost their jobs and their savings. Your administration has tried to stop the Depression by passing many new laws in banking, agriculture, and industry. Most of the new laws have helped businesses. If business improves, there

should be more work and more money for all Americans.

After three years, there are still more than 10 million workers without jobs. Many of them have no money to pay for food and rent. If the Depression continues, how will they survive? Is it the government's job to solve social problems? What should the government do to help?

© 1997 J. Weston Walch, Publisher

Name _____ Date _____

President Roosevelt: What should the government do to help poor people during the Depression? *(continued)*

Comprehension

1. Who are you in this decision?

2. How long have you been president?

3. When is the next presidential election?

4. How has the national government tried to stop the Depression?

5. How many American workers are unemployed?

6. In paragraph 2, what does the word <u>they</u> refer to?

7. What will happen to you if your administration does not stop the Depression?

Decision

- *What should the government do to help poor people during the Depression? Choose one or more of the following options:*

    (a) Do nothing. It is not the government's job to solve social problems.

    (b) Continue to help businesses.

    (c) Create new jobs for poor people.

    (d) Give money to poor people.

    (e) Give food to poor people.

    (f) Give houses to poor people.

    (g) Give land to poor people.

    (h) Ask people to move to another country where there are more jobs.

    (i) Other: _____

- *Why did you decide that way? Plan how you will explain your decision to your classmates. Write out your reasoning completely.*

American Citizens
Should the U.S. get involved in World War II?

It is 1940. You are an American citizen. Another world war has started in Africa, Asia, and Europe. In Africa, the country of Ethiopia has been conquered by the Italian army. In Asia, the Japanese now control Laos, Cambodia, Vietnam, and parts of China. The German Führer, Adolf Hitler, wants to conquer all of Europe. In only a few months, German soldiers have defeated the armies of Belgium, Czechoslovakia, Holland, France, and Poland. German airplanes have bombed cities in Spain and England, and the newspapers report that the German military is arresting and imprisoning Jewish people all across Europe.

Twenty-five years ago, we helped our allies win the Great War. More than 115,000 American soldiers were killed in that war, and more than 200,000 were wounded. We said that we would never get involved in another foreign war. Now Italy, Japan, and Germany are fighting against countries that are friendly to the United States. Our allies want us to help them win this war, too.

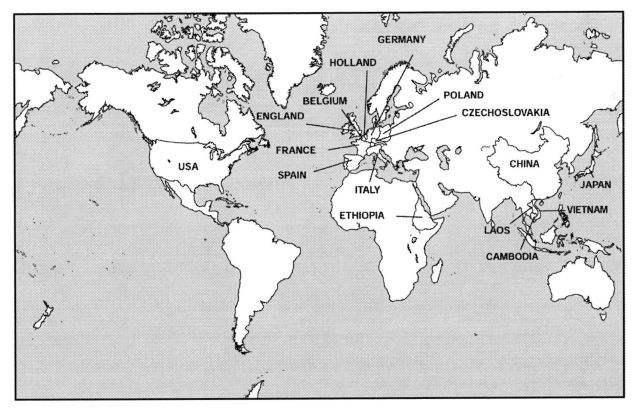

American Citizens: Should the U.S. get involved in World War II?
(continued)

Comprehension

1. Who are you in this decision?

2. Is this war happening on U.S. territory?

3. In paragraph 2, what does the word <u>them</u> refer to?

4. If we join this war, whom will we be fighting against?

5. Who are our allies? How do we know?

6. What are some reasons for entering this war?

7. What are some reasons for not entering this war?

Decision

● *What should the U.S. do about this war in Europe? Choose as many options as you think are necessary:*

    (a) We should not get involved in this war in any way.

    (b) We should stop selling U.S. products to Italy, Germany, and Japan.

    (c) We should stop buying Italian, German, and Japanese products.

    (d) We should sell weapons to our allies.

    (e) We should lend money to our allies.

    (f) We should begin preparing our country for war immediately.

    (g) We should join the war only if another country attacks us.

    (h) We should support whoever wins the war.

    (i) We should join the war now.

    (j) Other: _____

● *Why did you decide that way? Plan how you will explain your decision to your classmates. Write out your reasoning completely.*

American Citizens

1942

Are Japanese Americans and other immigrants dangerous to our national security?

It is January 1942. You are an American citizen. The U.S. is fighting in another world war, this time against Germany, Italy, and Japan. American soldiers are fighting and dying in Europe, Asia, and the Pacific.

America is a country of immigrants. Many of them come from the countries we are fighting now. Will German Americans, Italian Americans, and Japanese Americans be loyal to the U.S. during this war? Will they try to help their former countries, our enemies?

Some people believe that the government should not trust some of the immigrants. They say that some immigrants love their old countries more than they love America. The mayor of New York City, Fiorella La Guardia, says that German and Italian immigrants are loyal to the U.S., but he does not say anything about the Japanese Americans. Many people believe that the Japanese Americans living on the West Coast might not be loyal. They are different from the European immigrants. They look different and have a different language. Their religion is different, too. Maybe they will try to help

Japan attack our country!

Other people say that this is a crazy idea. The first Japanese immigrants came here as farmers almost 60 years ago. Most of the Japanese Americans were born in the U.S. and are American citizens. Many of them have volunteered to fight against Japan in the war.

Fiorella La Guardia

Name _____ Date _____

American Citizens: Are Japanese Americans and other immigrants dangerous to our national security? *(continued)*

Comprehension

1. Who are you in this decision?

2. Who is the U.S. fighting against?

3. Why are people talking about immigrants from Germany, Italy, and Japan?

4. Where do most Japanese Americans live in the U.S?

5. How are Japanese Americans different from other immigrants?

6. What do you think the question to decide about will be?

Decision

● *Should the U.S. government treat immigrants differently during the war? Choose one or more of the following options:*

    (a) No. The government should treat immigrants the same as everyone else.

    (b) The government should treat _____ immigrants differently.

    (c) The government should make _____ immigrants sign a loyalty oath to the United States.

    (d) The government should put_____immigrants into special camps.

    (e) The government should force _____ immigrants to serve in the military.

    (f) The government should not allow_____ to serve in the military.

    (g) The government should arrest the immigrants who are not U.S. citizens.

    (h) Other: _____

● *Why did you decide that way? Plan how you will explain your decision to your classmates. Write out your reasoning completely.*

1945

American Citizens
Should the U.S. join the United Nations?

It is June 1945. You are an American citizen. Germany has surrendered. Japan continues to fight. This second world war has lasted more than six years. Seventy million soldiers from 26 countries have fought, and 16 million soldiers have died. Eighteen million civilians have died. Millions more have been wounded and are missing. The war has cost trillions of dollars.

In San Francisco, delegates from 50 nations have been meeting. They have planned an international organization called the United Nations. One purpose of the U.N. is to avoid wars in the future. All peace-loving nations in the world can join. When they have disagreements, they can talk about them. Another purpose of the U.N. is to raise the standard of living around the world.

The delegates have written a charter that tells the rules of the United Nations. There will be several parts in the U.N. All nations will be in the General Assembly. In the General Assembly, nations can discuss all problems and recommend solutions. There will be a Security Council. Its job will be to solve international disagreements. The Security Council can create an international police force to keep peace if necessary. There will be an International Court of Justice. Countries that have disagreements with other countries can try to settle their problems in court. There will also be an Economic and Social Council. It will sponsor economic development in poor countries and human rights everywhere.

It has taken a long time to make plans that everyone can agree with. There have been many compromises to make everyone happy with the plan. Now each country must decide if it wants to join the U.N.

Of course, most people in America like the idea of the United Nations. Everyone wants peace. Some Americans do not want the United States to join the U.N., however. The plan gives the U.S.S.R. three votes in the General Assembly. This is because the U.S.S.R. is so worried that the United States and all our allies will control the U.N. Why should the U.S.S.R. have three votes if the U.S. has only one? And why should the U.S. have only one vote, like the small and weak countries? Also, some Americans do not like the U.N. having a police force. They do not want the United States to give troops to the U.N. Joining the U.N. would mean that the United States could not make its own decisions. They believe the United States should continue to be, as President Roosevelt said, the police force for the world.

Now the Senate must decide if the United States will join. How do you want the Senate to vote?

United Nations flag

American Citizens: Should the U.S. join the United Nations? *(continued)*

Comprehension

1. Who are you in this story?

2. Has World War II ended yet?

3. What are two reasons for creating the United Nations?

4. Which part of the U.N. will help poor countries develop?

5. Which part of the U.N. will be able to create a police force and send it to a trouble spot in the world?

6. What countries will be in the General Assembly?

7. What do Americans like about the U.N.?

8. What don't some Americans like about the U.N.?

9. Do you think small, weak countries would like the U.N.? Why?

10. Why would large countries like the U.N.?

11. For each statement, write *T* for true or *F* for false:

    (a) The superpowers wrote the United Nations plan.
    (b) All Americans want the U.S. to join the U.N.
    (c) One purpose of the U.N. is to prevent wars.
    (d) If people talk about problems, maybe they will not go to war.
    (e) The U.S. will have fewer votes in the General Assembly than the U.S.S.R.
    (f) The U.S. will have the most power in the Security Council.
    (g) The U.S. will have the same number of votes in the General Assembly as small, weak countries.
    (h) The U.N. will be able to use the American military.
    (i) The United States has to join the United Nations.

Decision

● *Should the U.S. join the United Nations? Choose one of the following options:*

    (a) Yes. Join the United Nations.
    (b) No. Do not join the United Nations.
    (c) Other: _____

● *Why did you decide that way? Plan how you will explain your decision to your classmates. Write out your reasoning completely.*

1945

President Truman

Should the U.S. drop the atomic bomb on Japan to end the war?

It is August 1945. You are President Harry Truman. World War II is almost over. The fighting in Europe stopped a few months ago, but it is continuing in Asia and the Pacific Ocean. Most of the fighting there is between U.S. and Japanese soldiers. The Soviet Union has promised to help the U.S. if Japan does not surrender soon. The Japanese know they are losing the war, but they have not surren-

President Harry Truman

dered. It looks as if the fighting will continue for several more months.

The Japanese government wants peace and will surrender, but only under certain conditions: (1) the Emperor will continue to rule Japan, and (2) the U.S. cannot rule Japan. The U.S. wants the war to end, too, but we must make sure that the Japanese cannot have a powerful army again. The U.S. does not want the Soviet Union to become strong in Japan, either. How can the war be ended in a way that is best for the United States?

During the war, U.S. scientists have been working on a secret weapon, an atomic bomb. It is the most powerful and terrible weapon in the history of the world. Now the bomb is ready.

Should the U.S. use the atomic bomb on Japan? This would be a fast way to end the war. It would prevent more American soldiers from being killed and injured, and it would stop the Soviets from entering the war against Japan. This bomb has been used in tests, but never in war. We don't really know how powerful it is. We know that if we drop the atomic bomb on Japan, many Japanese people will die.

President Truman: Should the U.S. drop the atomic bomb on Japan to end the war? *(continued)*

Comprehension

1. Who are you in this decision?

2. Where has the war ended?

3. In paragraph 1, what does the word <u>there</u> refer to?

4. Why haven't the Japanese already surrendered?

5. In paragraph 4, what does the word <u>It</u> refer to?

   (a) the atomic bomb.

   (b) using the atomic bomb.

6. Why don't you want the Soviet Union to help fight the Japanese?

7. What do you know about the atomic bomb?

Decision

- *Should the U.S. drop the atomic bomb on Japan? Choose one or more of the following options:*

   (a) Don't drop the bomb. Accept Japan's surrender under their conditions.

   (b) Don't drop the bomb. Begin an allied attack on Japan together with the Soviets.

   (c) Don't drop the bomb. Keep fighting and hope Japan will surrender without conditions.

   (d) Drop the atomic bomb on a part of Japan where nobody lives.

   (e) Drop the atomic bomb on a military target.

   (f) Drop the atomic bomb on a Japanese city.

   (g) Other: _____

- *Why did you decide that way? Plan how you will explain your decision to your classmates. Write out your reasoning completely.*

1947 | Truman Administration
Should America help rebuild Europe?

It is 1947. You are a member of President Truman's cabinet. World War II is over, but Europe, our most important trading partner, is a disaster. Millions of people died in the war. Whole cities and towns were wiped out, and houses, farms, factories, businesses, and banks were destroyed. Railroads, roads, and bridges were damaged, too. The European countries are slowly rebuilding, but it is going to take years to return to normal.

George Marshall was a U.S. general during the war. Now he is Secretary of State. Marshall says that the situation in Europe is much worse than most Americans understand. The Europeans cannot make the products they need. They cannot even grow enough food to feed themselves!

These problems in Europe are bad for America for three reasons. First, the European people do not have enough money to buy our products. Our factories will have to slow down and Americans will lose jobs. Second, the European governments are very unstable because of the bad economic situation. Socialism and communism are becoming popular in France and Italy. The Soviet Union is already too strong in Eastern Europe. Soon our enemies may control Western Europe, too. Third, we may need to put our soldiers in these countries someday. We have to think about the future. If we help Europe now, these countries will help us in the future. America must help Europe recover from the war. When we help Europe, we are helping America as well.

Not everyone agrees with Marshall's plan. We have a lot of problems here in America. If we give money to Europe, will there be enough money to pay for American schools, hospitals, and other projects? If the damage in Europe is as bad as Marshall says, it will cost billions of dollars to repair it. Can America afford to do this? Will these countries ever pay us back?

There are other problems, too. Which countries will get the money? During the war, Italy and Germany were our enemies. They killed thousands of American soldiers. Will we give money to these countries or only to our allies during the war? What about the Soviets and the territories they have taken, such as Poland and Czechoslovakia? These countries are in Europe, but they have communist governments. President Truman says they are our enemies now. Will Marshall's plan give them money, too? Finally, what about Japan? The United States dropped atomic bombs on Hiroshima and Nagasaki. Three hundred thousand Japanese civilians died because of our bombs. These two cities are totally destroyed. Will we give money to rebuild Japan?

Henry Wallace, the former Secretary of Agriculture, says this plan could get America into another war. The Soviet Union does not want the U.S. to become too powerful in Europe. This plan could lead us to war with the Soviet Union. Wallace says that the U.S. should take care of its own problems now. We lost more than 100,000 soldiers in World War I and more than 400,000 in World War II. We should stop thinking so much about Europe and think more about America.

Name _____ Date _____

Truman Administration: Should America help rebuild Europe?
(continued)

Comprehension

1. Who are you in this decision?

2. Why does Marshall want the U.S. to give money to Europe? Give four reasons.

3. What European countries fought against us in World War II?

4. Who is against Marshall's plan? What are his reasons?

Decision

● *What should America do to help Europe rebuild? Choose one or more of the following options:*

(a) We should loan money, not give it away for free.

(b) We should give money away, but only to those countries that were our allies during the war.

(c) We should give money to the countries that need it the most.

(d) We should give money to the countries that lost the war.

(e) Some European countries already owe us money. Forgive these loans.

(f) Lower the taxes on European products so Americans will buy them.

(g) Sell some American goods more cheaply in Europe. Which goods?

Devastation of World War II

_____

(h) Give weapons to European countries.

(i) Do nothing to help European countries rebuild.

(j) Other: _____

● *Why did you decide that way? Plan how you will explain your decision to your classmates. Write out your reasoning completely.*

U.S. Farm Owners

1948

How can we get cheap labor to work on our farms?

It is 1948. You are an American farm owner. The population of the United States is growing quickly. More food is needed to feed all these people. Who is going to grow it?

Agriculture in the U.S. is changing. Today, most people live in cities, not on farms. There are fewer farms, but they are much larger than they used to be. In the past, people and animals did all the work on farms. Now, tractors and other special machines do most farmwork. However, machines cannot pick fruit and vegetables as well as human workers can.

During harvest time, the farm owners need hundreds of workers to pick and pack the crops. But the harvest only lasts a few weeks. When all the fruit and vegetables are in boxes, the owners do not need the workers anymore until the next harvest.

Farming is a business now. The farm owners need a special kind of worker. <u>They</u> want people who will work very hard for a short time and then leave after the harvest.

They want to pay as little as possible and give no insurance or other benefits. Most Americans do not want to do this work for such low wages and no benefits.

A few years ago, when many Americans were fighting in World War II, we needed temporary workers. The federal government invited thousands of Mexican workers to work on American farms. When the war ended, many of these workers stayed here. Now they are telling their families to come to the United States. In Mexico, there are few jobs and the wages are low. Farmworkers can make more money working here.

The farm owners make bigger profits using Mexican farmworkers. Consumers benefit, too. Because the workers are paid less, Americans pay lower prices for fruit and vegetables. But this system is supporting illegal immigration because many of the Mexican farmworkers did not enter this country legally. Is this the best way to grow America's food?

Mexicans packing crops

U.S. Farm Owners: How can we get cheap labor to work on our farms? *(continued)*

Comprehension

1. Who are you in this story?

2. In paragraph 4, what does the word <u>They</u> refer to?

3. How is farming different today?

4. Why don't the farm owners want to give workers insurance?

5. Has the U.S. ever used Mexican workers before? When?

6. Most Americans don't want to do farmwork. Why do many Mexicans want these bad jobs?

Decision

- *What should we do? Choose one or more of the following options:*

    (a) Pay higher wages to attract more American workers.

    (b) Make farms smaller again, so we don't need so many workers.

    (c) Develop new machines to pick fruit and vegetables.

    (d) Invite Mexican workers to come, but only for the harvest.

    (e) Invite Mexican workers to stay in the U.S. if they work only on farms.

    (f) Invite workers from other countries.

    (g) Other: _____

- *Why did you decide that way? Plan how you will explain your decision to your classmates. Write out your reasoning completely.*

President Truman

1950

Should the United States fight communism in Korea?

It is 1950. You are President Harry Truman. North Korea has just invaded South Korea. At the end of World War II, Korea was divided into two parts by the U.S. and the U.S.S.R. Now the North Koreans want to reunite the North and South under one communist government. The two strongest communist countries, the U.S.S.R and China, want this, too.

The North Korean army is very strong, because the Soviets have given them guns and tanks. The South Korean army, however, is weak. South Korea is asking the United States and the United Nations for help. It would be easy for us to send soldiers and weapons to help the South Koreans, but is this a good idea? If we help South Korea, maybe the Soviets or Chinese will send their soldiers, too. That could start another world war, this time with atomic bombs! Many U.S. soldiers and even civilians would die.

Should the U.S. help South Korea? Some military leaders want to help, but they would use only planes and ships instead of ground troops. This would save the lives of our soldiers, but it could start a war with the U.S.S.R. and China. Maybe we should wait

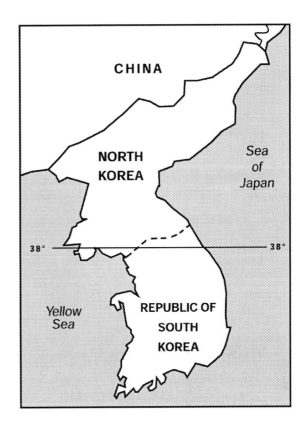

for the United Nations to decide. Then other countries could help us fight the North Koreans. Maybe we should do nothing. There are few American businesses or people in South Korea. The only reason to go there is to stop communism.

President Truman: Should the United States fight
communism in Korea? *(continued)*

Comprehension

1. Who are you in this decision?

2. Why are there two Koreas?

3. Who wants North and South Korea to have one communist government?

4. Why is Korea important to the United States?

5. Why is Korea important to the U.S.S.R.?

6. Where did the North Koreans get their weapons?

7. What are reasons for the U.S. to help South Korea?

8. What are reasons for the U.S. not to help South Korea?

Decision

● *What should the U.S. do about the North Korean invasion of South Korea? Choose all the actions you think we should take:*

(a) Do not help the South Koreans.

(b) Send the South Koreans money and guns, but not soldiers.

(c) Send American ships and planes to South Korea, but no soldiers.

(d) Drop an atomic bomb on North Korea.

(e) Tell the Soviets and Chinese to stay out of Korea.

(f) Wait for the United Nations to decide what to do.

(g) Send soldiers and supplies to South Korea.

(h) Other: _____

● *Why did you decide that way? Plan how you will explain your decision to your classmates. Write out your reasoning completely.*

1950

State Department Worker
What should you tell the Senate Foreign Relations Committee?

It is 1950. You are a government employee in the State Department. Today there is a message for you at your office. The Senate Foreign Relations Committee wants to question you about your political beliefs. Committee members want to know your ideas about communism and the Communist Party. They might ask you questions about your friends and the people you work with.

Many Americans are afraid of communism. The Soviet Union and China, two of the largest countries in the world, have communist governments. The Soviets even have the atomic bomb. A Republican senator from Wisconsin, Joseph McCarthy, says that communism is America's greatest enemy. He believes that the government does not pay enough attention to the spread of communism inside America. China had a communist revolution last year. McCarthy says that the State Department knew <u>it</u> was going to happen but did not tell anyone. McCarthy says he has proof that there are over 200 communists working in the State Department. He says your name is one of those on his list!

There are strong state and national laws to punish communists. Communists can be fined and sent to jail. Even people who are only accused of being communists have lost their jobs and businesses. You are not a communist, but you know some people who

<u>are</u>. You also know some people who are not communists but who like some of the Communist party's ideas. You must appear before the committee or you could go to jail. You do not have to answer the committee's questions, however. The Fifth Amendment says that Americans can refuse to answer a question. But, if you do this, the committee might think you are trying to hide something. The First Amendment protects Americans' freedom of speech. But now the government is punishing people for their ideas!

Senator Joseph McCarthy makes a point

The message says that you should appear before the Senate committee next week. Your job and your reputation could depend on how you answer the committee's questions. Anyone you talk about could also be questioned by the committee.

State Department Worker: What should you tell the Senate Foreign Relations Committee? *(continued)*

Comprehension

1. Who are you in this decision?

2. Who is Joseph McCarthy?

3. Why is your name on McCarthy's list?

4. In paragraph 2, what does the word <u>it</u> refer to?

5. In paragraph 3, what does the word <u>are</u> refer to?

6. What will happen if you do not appear before the committee?

7. What might happen if you plead the Fifth Amendment?

8. Why do you think McCarthy is attacking the State Department?

9. Which Amendment says that Americans can say what they believe?

Decision

● *What should you tell the committee? Choose one or more of the following options:*

    (a) Tell them nothing. Do not appear before the committee.

    (b) Tell them nothing. Leave the country before the hearing.

    (c) Refuse to answer any questions. Plead the Fifth Amendment.

    (d) Answer each question truthfully, but do not give any names.

    (e) Answer everything the committee asks, including names.

    (f) Tell the committee you cannot remember.

    (g) Give the committee false information.

    (h) Other: _____

● *Why did you decide that way? Plan how you will explain your decision to your classmates. Write out your reasoning completely.*

1954

Supreme Court
Should America have segregated schools?

It is 1954. You are a justice on the Supreme Court. You are deciding if states have the right to have separate schools for blacks and whites.

Many southern states have separate public facilities for whites and blacks. Schools, hospitals, bus stations, and even bathrooms and drinking fountains are segregated. Segregation means "separation": one facility for black people and another for white people.

In 1896, the Supreme Court said that segregation was constitutional, but only if the black and white facilities were equal. The Court decided that it was all right for southern states to have separate railroad cars, but only if the cars for blacks and whites were the same. Now "separate but equal" is common in the southern states.

In Topeka, Kansas, black parents are angry about segregated schools. They say that Negro schools are not as good as white schools, because the state government of Kansas gives white schools more money. These parents say that separate is not equal. The bad conditions in black schools are hurting Negro children. They want the government to make one good school system for blacks and whites together.

Many white parents disagree. They want segregated schools. They do not want their children to go to school with black children. They say that the states have the right to choose segregation. They do not want the federal government to tell the states what to do.

Is segregation good for America? Should the states have the right to segregate schools?

Segregated classroom of the 1950's

Supreme Court: Should America have segregated schools? *(continued)*

Comprehension

1. Do you think the Supreme Court justices are black or white?

2. What does "separate but equal" mean?

3. What did the court say about segregation in 1896?

4. What things are segregated in southern states?

5. What do black parents in Topeka want? Why?

6. Who favors segregated schools? What are their reasons? _____

_____

7. Can the Supreme Court change its mind?

Decision

● *Is segregation in education good for America? Choose one of the following options:*

    (a) No. Schools should not be regulated in any state.

    (b) Segregated schools and other public facilities are all right, but they must truly
        be equal. How will you guarantee that the schools for black students are as

        good as the schools for white students? _____

        _____

    (c) The Constitution does not say anything about this question. The national
        government may not tell the states how to run their schools.

    (d) Other: _____

● *Why did you decide that way? Plan how you will explain your decision to your classmates.*
Write out your reasoning completely.

1955

Negroes in Montgomery, Alabama
Should we join the bus boycott?

It is December 1955. You are a Negro living in Montgomery, Alabama. Many Negroes ride the city buses to work. In fact, most of the riders on the buses are Negroes. But the seats on the buses are segregated. That means that the Negroes have to sit in the back of the bus. Only white people can sit in the front. If a Negro is sitting in the front of the bus, a white person can make the Negro stand up and move to the back. The law in Alabama says that public transportation must be segregated like this.

A few days ago, Rosa Parks, a Negro woman, refused to give up her seat to a white man. She was arrested. She is going to be tried in court tomorrow. Negro leaders in

Montgomery have called for a boycott of city buses. They think that now is a good time to protest against state laws that allow segregation. Last year, the Supreme Court decided that school segregation is unconstitutional. Maybe we can make segregated transportation illegal, too.

But a boycott could be dangerous. White people will be angry. The police will not protect Negroes. There will be violence against us. Nobody knows if a boycott will change the law. There have been boycotts in other states, but the laws have not changed. In addition, we will have to walk to work, pay for taxis, or ride with friends who have cars. Life will be more difficult. Is it worth it?

Fingerprinting Rosa Parks

1955

Negroes in Montgomery, Alabama: Should we join the bus boycott?
(continued)

Comprehension

1. Who are you in this situation?

2. Why do Negroes want to change the state law?

3. Why do the state laws say that bus seats must be segregated?

4. What do Negro leaders think is a good way to change the state laws?

5. Why do they think that now is a good time to try to change the public transportation laws?

6. How could a bus boycott change the state law?

7. What are some good reasons for joining the boycott?

8. What are some good reasons for not joining the boycott?

9. What does the last sentence of the story ("Is it worth it?") mean?

10. What decision do you have to make?

Decision

- *Should you join the bus boycott? Choose one of the following options:*

    (a) Yes, join the bus boycott.

    (b) No, do not join the bus boycott.

    (c) Do not join the boycott the first day. Wait for a while.

    How long will you wait? _____

    How will you decide to join or not to join? _____

    _____

    (d) Other: _____

- *Why did you decide that way? Plan how you will explain your decision to your classmates. Write out your reasoning completely.*

U.S. Congress

1961
Should we spend more money on space exploration?

It is 1961. You are a member of Congress. President Kennedy wants the national government to spend more money to explore outer space. Kennedy says that the U.S. space program is far behind the Soviet Union's program. We know that the Soviets are building a new kind of rocket that will land on the moon someday! President Kennedy says that we should get there first. He is asking the Congress to put more money in the budget for space exploration.

Should we spend more on space? Some Americans agree with the president. Space exploration is good for America. In space, we can learn about the earth and other planets. We can develop new technology that will help Americans live better. The new technology for space exploration could be used by the American military, too. There could be valuable minerals on the moon. Maybe we could bring these minerals to Earth and use them here. Besides, we need to keep up with the Soviet Union. If the Soviet rocket lands on the moon first, the United States will be behind in the space race.

Other Americans disagree with the president. They say that we should spend our money to solve America's problems. In many parts of our country, people need better schools, hospitals, roads, and other public services. We should spend this money to solve these problems. Knowing about space is not as important as helping people now.

Or should we spend money
to solve America's problems?

U.S. Congress: Should we spend more money on space exploration?

(continued)

Comprehension

1. Who are you in this decision?

2. Why does President Kennedy want to spend more money on space exploration?

3. What other country has a space program?

4. Why do some Americans oppose spending more on space?

5. For each statement, write *F* for fact or *O* for opinion. Remember that facts are things that can be checked and agreed to by everyone. Opinions are a person's own ideas.

   (a) The Soviet rocket will land on the moon before the American rocket.

   (b) There are valuable minerals on the moon.

   (c) We are not spending enough money on space exploration now.

   (d) Some Americans agree with President Kennedy.

   (e) Knowing about space is not as important as helping people.

Decision

● *Should we spend more on space exploration? Choose one of the following options:*

   (a) No. First we should solve our problems here in America.

   (b) President Kennedy is right. We should spend more on space exploration.

   (c) Other: _____

● *Why did you decide that way? Plan how you will explain your decision to your classmates. Write out your reasoning completely.*

1961

President Kennedy
Should the U.S. invade Cuba?

It is 1961. You are the new president, John F. Kennedy. There is a foreign policy decision to make. What should the United States do about the new government of Cuba?

The island of Cuba is only 90 miles south of Florida. For years, the United States was friendly with Cuba. Wealthy Americans owned businesses and took vacations there. Three years ago, Cuba had a revolution. The new government took land and businesses away from the richest Cubans. The government kept some of these properties and gave others to poor Cubans. Most people in Cuba are happy about this, but the wealthy people who lost their property are very angry at the new government. Many of them left Cuba and live in Florida now.

Now the Cuban government is taking land and property that belong to American companies. The Cuban leader, Fidel Castro, says that these properties belong to the people of Cuba. Castro has just signed a trade agreement with the Soviet Union, a communist country. Will Cuba become communist, too? We do not want a communist country as a neighbor.

Your predecessor, President Eisenhower, had a secret plan to invade Cuba. Under this plan, the U.S. government trained 1,500 Cuban exiles as soldiers. These exiles say that the people in Cuba are becoming unhappy with Castro's government. If the U.S. supports this invasion with guns and planes,

the Cuban people will join the fight against Castro. If the invasion is successful, there will be a new government in Cuba—one that is friendly to the United States.

Fidel Castro

Invading Cuba could be good for American business. It would also show the Soviet Union that the U.S. does not want communism in the Americas. We invaded Guatemala in 1954 because they had a socialist government. Now the government there is friendly to the U.S.

On the other hand, other countries might object. Both the U.S. and Cuba belong to the Organization of American States. We promised not to attack each other or to interfere in each other's governments. This invasion would be illegal.

President Kennedy: Should the U.S. invade Cuba? *(continued)*

Comprehension

1. Who are you in this decision?

2. In what year did Cuba have a revolution?

3. Why is the Cuban government unpopular in the U.S.?

4. What makes you think that Cuba might become communist?

5. Who made the plan to invade Cuba?

6. Who supports this invasion?

7. Why did some people leave Cuba?

8. Were the exiles soldiers when they left Cuba?

9. Why did the U.S. invade Guatemala? What changed after that invasion? Why is that important now?

10. What could happen if the invasion of Cuba is successful?

11. What could happen if the invasion fails?

Decision

● *The plan is ready to go. Should the U.S. invade Cuba? Choose one of the following options:*

    (a) Yes

    (b) No

    (c) Other: _____

● *Why did you decide that way? Plan how you will explain your decision to your classmates. Write out your reasoning completely.*

Name _____   Date _____

President Kennedy
What should the U.S. do about the Soviet missiles in Cuba?

It is 1962. You are President John F. Kennedy. The U.S. is having more trouble with Cuba. This time it is worse than ever. American spy planes have taken photographs of nuclear missile bases being built in Cuba. We know that the Soviet Union is building these bases.

A few minutes ago, our planes found Soviet ships carrying nuclear missiles to Cuba! If they are delivered, Cuba could attack American cities—such as New York and Washington—very suddenly someday.

What should you do? Your advisers have several ideas. Some want to surround Cuba with U.S. ships. This blockade will stop the Soviet ships from delivering the missiles. Others want to order the Soviet ships to return to the Soviet Union if they do not want a war. Some advisers say we should try to make a deal with the Soviet leader, Nikita Khrushchev. He wants us to remove the U.S. nuclear missiles from Turkey, on the Soviet border. He also wants us to promise that we will not attack Cuba if the Soviet Union removes its missiles there.

The Soviet ships are getting closer. If we don't do something in the next few hours, there could be a nuclear war between the U.S. and the Soviet Union. Millions of people could die. What should our government do?

Photo of Cuban missile site taken from the air

President Kennedy: What should the U.S. do about the Soviet missiles in Cuba? *(continued)*

Comprehension

1. Who are you in this decision?
2. How did you learn about the Soviet missile bases in Cuba?
3. Where are the missiles now?
4. In paragraph 2, what does the word <u>they</u> refer to?
5. What does Khrushchev want the U.S. to do?
6. In paragraph 3, what does the word <u>Others</u> refer to?
7. Find these places on the classroom map: Cuba, New York, Washington, the Soviet Union, and Turkey.
8. Why are nuclear missiles in Cuba dangerous for the U.S.?
9. For each statement, write *F* for fact or *O* for opinion. Remember that facts are things that can be checked and agreed to by everyone. Opinions are a person's own ideas.
   (a) Cuba will use the missiles to attack American cities.
   (b) If our ships blockade Cuba, there will be a war between the U.S. and the U.S.S.R.
   (c) The Soviet ships will arrive in Cuba soon if we do not act fast to stop them.
   (d) The Soviet Union is building these bases in Cuba.
   (e) Khrushchev wants us to remove U.S. nuclear missiles in Turkey.

Decision

● *What should the U.S. do about the Soviet missiles in Cuba? Choose one or more of the following options:*

   (a) Invade Cuba now.
   (b) Talk to Khrushchev and try to make peace.
   (c) Warn Khrushchev that the U.S. will attack the Soviet Union if its ships do not turn around and return home.
   (d) Use U.S. ships to blockade Cuba.
   (e) Attack the Soviet ships carrying the missiles.
   (f) Attack the Soviet Union.
   (g) Promise not to invade Cuba.
   (h) Promise to remove our nuclear missiles from Turkey.
   (i) Promise to destroy all our nuclear missiles if the Soviet Union does the same.
   (j) Other: _____

● *Why did you decide that way? Plan how you will explain your decision to your classmates. Write out your reasoning completely.*

Migrant Farmworkers

1962

How can we get better working conditions?

It is 1962. We are migrant farmworkers in California. We do not own the land we work on. We pick fruits and vegetables on other people's farms. When we finish working on one farm, we go to work on a different one.

Most of us are from Mexico. Some of us have a legal right to be in the United States, and some of us came here illegally. We have been coming to work in the U.S. for many years because there are not enough jobs in Mexico. The American farm owners need us. They cannot find enough Americans to do this work.

The working conditions and pay are bad. Picking fruit and vegetables is hard. Sometimes we work for 10 or 12 hours a day. The farm owners own the houses we live in and the stores where we buy food. The rent and prices are too high, but there are no other places to live or to shop!

Some of these working conditions are illegal, but how can we improve them? If we complain, we could lose our jobs. If the owners tell the government that we are here illegally, we could be sent back to Mexico. Some workers say we should organize a union for farmworkers. In a union, all the workers could join together to have power. We could demand better wages and working conditions. If the owners refuse to give us these things,

we will refuse to work. We can ask other Americans not to buy products from these owners. We need to organize ourselves.

Other people say we will get into trouble if we have a union. The farm owners will not agree to it. They will not hire people who are in the union. The owners are more powerful than we are, so we must be careful.

Living conditions of migrant farmworkers

Migrant Farmworkers: How can we get better working conditions?
(continued)

Comprehension

1. Who are we in this decision?

2. In paragraph 1, what does the word <u>one</u> refer to?

3. Who owns the land where you work?

4. Why are you living and working in the United States?

5. Why do you say the working conditions are bad?

6. Why are some farmworkers afraid to complain?

7. Is there a union for farmworkers now?

8. What can a union do to help you?

9. What problems could you have if you start a union?

Decision

● *How can farmworkers get better working conditions? Chose one or more of the following options:*

   (a) Do nothing. Keep working the way we are.

   (b) Don't start a union. Tell the farm owners that we want better conditions.

   (c) Start a union of farmworkers to represent us.

   (d) Go on strike. We won't work until we get better conditions.

   (e) Ask consumers not to buy the farm owners' products until we get better conditions.

   (f) Look for different work in the United States.

   (g) Go back to Mexico to look for work.

   (h) Other: _____

● *Why did you decide that way? Plan how you will explain your decision to your classmates. Write out your reasoning completely.*

Police Officer
What rights do people have if they are accused of a crime?

1963

It is 1963. You are a police officer in Arizona. You have arrested a 23-year-old man, Ernesto Miranda. You have charged him with kidnapping and raping an 18-year-old woman. You are talking with him in the police station now. You are asking him questions. He is answering all your questions. At first, he said he did not kidnap and rape the woman. But now you think he is lying.

You know that the Bill of Rights has rules about people when they are arrested. Accused people have the right to have a lawyer with them during questioning by the police. <u>They</u> do not have to answer questions that prove they are guilty. They do not have to say they are guilty. They have the right to know that you can tell the court anything they say to you.

But you think that Miranda will admit that he committed the crime. If you question him carefully, he will probably tell you he did it. Maybe you can even get him to write it on paper!

Should you tell him about the rights he has? <u>They</u> are written in the Bill of Rights.

Anyone can read them. He should know his rights. It is not your job to tell him. Your job is to arrest him for his crime. If you can get him to say he raped and kidnapped the woman, you can get one criminal into prison. You can make the city safer.

Ernesto Miranda

Police Officer: What rights do people have if they are accused of a crime? *(continued)*

Comprehension

1. Who are you in this story?

2. Why have you arrested Mr. Miranda?

3. Where are you now?

4. What does the word <u>They</u> refer to in the second paragraph?

5. What are <u>They</u> in the fourth paragraph?

6. What rights does Mr. Miranda have?

7. Why haven't you told him his rights yet?

8. What do you want him to do?

9. What decision do you have to make?

Decision

● *What should you do? Choose one of the following options:*

   (a) Tell him his rights.

   (b) Do not tell him his rights. Try to get him to admit that he committed the crime.

   (c) Ask him if he knows his rights.

        If he says yes, _____

        If he says no, _____

   (d) Other: _____

● *Why did you decide that way? Plan how you will explain your decision to your classmates. Write out your reasoning completely.*

Name _____   Date _____

1963

Negro College Students
Whom should we follow—Martin Luther King or Malcolm X?

It is 1963. We are Negro college students in Alabama. The United States is changing in many ways, but we still do not have the same rights as white people. Negroes have lived in America for 350 years. Slavery has been illegal for 100 years. The United States government has done some things to help us get our civil rights, but only when we demand them. If we want to get all our rights, we have to be organized.

Dr. Martin Luther King, Jr.

What is the best way to get our civil rights? Dr. Martin Luther King, Jr., a minister from Atlanta, says that nonviolence is the only way. This means demanding our rights in a peaceful way. If the white people use violence against us, we do not fight back. But we keep demanding our rights. Sometimes, Negroes demanding civil rights are attacked

by angry white people. In Birmingham, Alabama, we tried to register to vote. The police used dogs and fire hoses against us. White people control the police departments and the army. Dr. King says that if we are violent, many Negroes will be hurt or killed. He says only love and tolerance can conquer racism. A lot of people agree.

Malcolm X

Malcolm X, a Muslim leader from the North, says that nonviolence will not stop discrimination against Negroes. He says we must educate ourselves. We should buy everything from black-owned businesses. We should not pollute our minds and bodies with drugs and alcohol. We should learn to defend ourselves and to fight back if white people attack us. A lot of people think that Malcolm X is right.

1963

Negro College Students: Whom should we follow—Martin Luther King or Malcolm X? *(continued)*

Comprehension

1. Who are we in this decision?

2. When has the federal government helped us get our civil rights?

3. What does Malcolm X mean by "we must educate ourselves"?

4. What does Dr. King want us to do if whites attack us?

5. What does Malcolm X believe about using violence?

6. For each statement, write *T* for true and *F* for false:

    (a) Negroes control the police departments and the army in the U.S.

    (b) Dr. King believes that violence causes more violence.

    (c) Both Dr. King and Malcolm X are religious leaders.

    (d) Malcolm X says that Negroes should attack whites.

Decision

● *Whom should we follow—Malcolm X or Martin Luther King? Choose one of the following options:*

    (a) Malcolm X

    (b) Martin Luther King

    (c) Other: _____

● *Why did you decide that way? Plan how you will explain your decision to your classmates. Write out your reasoning completely.*

Which leader do you think most white people like better—Dr. King or Malcolm X?

Why do you think so? _____

_____

Why does this matter? _____

_____

President Johnson

1964

What is the government's role in fighting poverty?

It is 1964. You are President Lyndon B. Johnson. The United States is the richest country in the world. We have more cars, radios, televisions, and telephones than any other country. Our factories are producing more products than ever before.

But some Americans are not getting richer. A government report says that 20 percent of Americans live in poverty. One out of every five Americans has difficulty paying for food, clothing, housing, medical care, and transportation. Many of these poor people are children and senior citizens. Many of them live in slums. Education, nutrition, and health care programs would help <u>them</u>, but the state and local governments do not have money to do <u>these things</u>.

You are surprised that so many Americans live in poverty. Many people agree that

the federal government needs to help solve this problem. But what is the best way?

Child of poverty

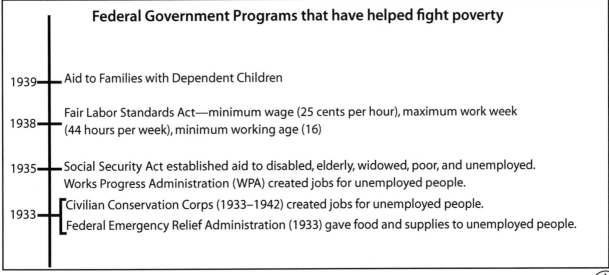

Federal Government Programs that have helped fight poverty

1939 — Aid to Families with Dependent Children

1938 — Fair Labor Standards Act—minimum wage (25 cents per hour), maximum work week (44 hours per week), minimum working age (16)

1935 — Social Security Act established aid to disabled, elderly, widowed, poor, and unemployed. Works Progress Administration (WPA) created jobs for unemployed people.

1933 — Civilian Conservation Corps (1933–1942) created jobs for unemployed people. Federal Emergency Relief Administration (1933) gave food and supplies to unemployed people.

© 1997 J. Weston Walch, Publisher

Name _____   Date _____

President Johnson: What is the government's role in
fighting poverty? *(continued)*

Comprehension

1. Who are you in this decision?
2. There are 150 million people in America. How many of them live in poverty?
3. Why are you surprised to learn that there is poverty in America?
4. In paragraph 2, what does the word <u>them</u> refer to?
5. In paragraph 2, what are <u>these things</u>?
6. Why don't the state and local governments fix the poverty problem?
7. What decision do you have to make?

Decision

● *How should the federal government fight poverty in America? Choose as many actions as you think we need to take:*

  (a) Cut government spending on the military and foreign aid. We can use this money to help poor people.
  (b) Lower taxes. People will have more money to buy things and start businesses.
  (c) Increase federal taxes. The federal government can use the extra money to help poor people.
  (d) Make health care free for all Americans.
  (e) Make college free for all Americans.
  (f) Loan government money to Americans who want to go to college.
  (g) Start free preschool programs for poor American children.
  (h) Build inexpensive public housing.
  (i) Pass a law that reduces the rent for all Americans.
  (j) Give poor people federal land to live on, or sell it cheap.
  (k) Build more roads, schools, hospitals, and other public facilities. This will create jobs for more Americans.
  (l) Build cheap public transportation.
  (m) Ask Americans to volunteer to help poor people.
  (n) Increase the national guaranteed minimum wage.
  (o) Give federal money to the state governments. Let them decide how to spend the money.
  (p) Ask states to increase taxes and take care of their own problems. Poverty is not the federal government's problem.
  (q) Give each poor American _____ dollars.
  (r) Other: _____

● *Why did you decide that way? Plan how you will explain your decision to your classmates. Write out your reasoning completely.*

U.S. Congress

1964

Should the U.S. fight communism in Vietnam?

It is August 7, 1964. You are a senator in the U.S. Congress. President Johnson says that a few days ago the North Vietnamese attacked American ships. He says that American planes are now attacking North Vietnam. He wants Congress to give him power to defend our ships and soldiers. He also wants Congress to give him special powers. He wants to have the power to do anything to help our allies in Southeast Asia fight for their freedom. The House of Representatives and the Senate have been debating this for two days.

Ten years ago, Vietnam won a war of independence from France, but Vietnam was divided into two separate parts. North Vietnam was communist, and South Vietnam was anticommunist. Fighting between the two countries started soon. The Soviet Union and China are helping North Vietnam. They are all communist, and they are our enemies. Our government believes that we must help our

friends fight against communism. If we do not help them fight, the communists will take over each of our friends one by one. Like dominoes, first South Vietnam, then Cambodia, and then Laos will fall. At first, the U.S. sent about 700 military advisers to help the South Vietnamese. Now, there are 21,000 American advisers there. Their job is to teach the South Vietnamese soldiers how to fight and use American weapons. However, we are not at war against North Vietnam. We are only helping South Vietnam fight against communism.

Some people say that we should not be involved in a foreign war. It is far away from us. We do not know how to fight a war in the jungles. It is a civil war that the Vietnamese should fight by themselves. Americans could die in this war. Sending them to Vietnam is costing our country millions of dollars. We could use this money here in America.

1964 — U.S. sent military advisers and equipment to support South Vietnam.

1960 — National Front for the Liberation of South Vietnam (NLF) formed and increased military activity against the government.

Vietminh in South Vietnam became communist Vietcong and organized antigovernment activities.

1954 — French surrendered. Peace talks and agreements temporarily divided Vietnam into two parts, North and South.

The French tried to regain control of Indochina, but Vietminh forces supported by China and the U.S.S.R. opposed them. U.S. sent $2 billion but no soldiers to help the French.

1945 — Japanese were defeated in World War II and gave up their control of Indochina.

U.S. Congress: Should the U.S. fight communism in Vietnam?
(continued)

Comprehension

1. Who are you in this story?
2. Who is fighting in this war?
3. What has Congress been debating for two days?
4. Who are our allies?
5. Who are our enemies?
6. Why are we helping South Vietnam in this war?
7. How have we helped South Vietnam so far?
8. Whom does <u>Their</u> refer to in the second paragraph?
9. What are some reasons not to fight in this war?
10. Where are the American ships that were attacked?
    (a) Near Vietnam.
    (b) Near the U.S.
11. Why do you think American planes are attacking North Vietnam?
12. What does President Johnson want?
13. What does the word <u>them</u> refer to in the last paragraph?
14. What decision does Congress have to make now?

Decision

● *Should Congress give President Johnson permission to send more soldiers, supplies, and money to fight against the communists in Southeast Asia? Choose one of the following options:*

    (a) Yes, give President Johnson all the power he needs to fight the communists.
    (b) No, do not give President Johnson this special power. Bring back our soldiers. Stop sending aid.
    (c) No, do not give President Johnson this special power. He should ask Congress for permission every time he wants to send aid.
    (d) Yes, give President Johnson special power for six months. Then we will decide again what to do.
    (e) No, do not give President Johnson this special power. First he should ask Congress to declare war. According to the Constitution, only the Congress can declare war.
    (f) No, do not give President Johnson this special power. We should ask the United Nations for permission.
    (g) Other: _____

● *Why did you decide that way? Plan how you will explain your decision to your classmates. Write out your reasoning completely.*

1965 ▽ Conscientious Objector?
What can you do if you oppose this war but your government wants you to fight?

It is 1965. You are a young man, 19 years old. The draft board has just sent you a letter. The letter orders you to join the military. Young men who are in school can wait to join the military, but you are not in school.

You do not want to join the military. Some men do not join the military because their religion says that killing is wrong. They are called conscientious objectors. But <u>that</u> is not your reason. You believe that some wars, such as wars to defend our country, are right.

But nobody is attacking our country.

You do not want to join the military because you think <u>this</u> war in Vietnam is wrong. The U.S. should not be fighting in Vietnam. This war is for the Vietnamese. It is a civil war. America has no business there. American supplies and soldiers are only making the war continue longer. Thousands of people are being killed and wounded. <u>The country</u> is being destroyed.

I WANT YOU
FOR U.S. ARMY
NEAREST RECRUITING STATION

© 1997 J. Weston Walch, Publisher

Name _____ Date _____

Comprehension

1. Who are you in this story?

2. What is the draft board's job?

3. Why does the draft board say that you have to join the military?

4. What are conscientious objectors?

5. What does <u>that</u> refer to in the second paragraph?

6. Why aren't you a conscientious objector according to the draft board?

7. Why don't you want to join the military now?

8. Are some wars good and some wars bad?

9. What does <u>The country</u> refer to in the last paragraph?

10. For each statement, write *F* for fact or *O* for opinion. Remember that facts are things that can be checked and agreed to by everyone. Opinions are a person's own ideas.

    (a) The Bible says that killing is wrong.

    (b) Some wars are right.

    (c) A war to defend your own country is all right.

    (d) The war in Vietnam is wrong.

    (e) If the government tells you to join the military, you should do it.

    (f) Thousands of people are being killed.

    (g) Conscientious objectors don't have to join the military.

Name _____ Date _____

Decision

- *What should you do? Choose one of the following options:*

    (a) Tell the draft board you are a conscientious objector. That means you are opposed to war for religious reasons. (You will have to prove that you have religious reasons against fighting in the war.)

    (b) Leave the U.S.A. Go to Canada. (If you do, the U.S.A. might never let you return to America.)

    (c) Tell the draft board you refuse to join the military. (You will be put in prison.)

    (d) When you go to the draft board, act crazy. Or say that you are a homosexual. Maybe they will not want you.

    (e) Cut off a finger or a toe. Friends tell you that handicapped men do not have to be in the military.

    (f) Join the military. Maybe they will not send you to Vietnam. If they send you to Vietnam, don't fight.

    (g) Tell the draft board you are a conscientious objector because you think *this* war is wrong. Ask the board to change its definition of a conscientious objector.

    (h) Tell the draft board that you are a pacifist and you think all wars are wrong.

    (i) Other: _____

- *Why did you decide that way? Plan how you will explain your decision to your classmates. Write out your reasoning completely.*

Vietnam War Protesters

How can we stop the war in Vietnam?

It is 1968. You are an American citizen. The U.S. has been fighting a war in Vietnam for more than four years, and you do not like it. You believe it is wrong for the U.S. to be in this war.

At first, you believed what the government told you. You thought it was important to fight communism. Communism would take over the world if we did not fight <u>it</u> in small countries like Vietnam.

Now, you are beginning to oppose the war. You want to believe the government, but you are beginning to distrust what the leaders say. Every night on television, you see young American men and Vietnamese soldiers and civilians getting killed. Vietnam is being destroyed. The president keeps telling us that we are winning the war. But last January, the North Vietnamese won many battles and captured many cities.

You are beginning to agree with the Vietnam War protesters. Many of them are only college students, but some national leaders like Martin Luther King and Senators George McGovern, Eugene McCarthy, and Robert Kennedy also oppose the war. They say we should not be in this war. It is strange that the U.S. has never called <u>this</u> a war! It seems that the U.S. is not really fighting hard. Why are we there? It is far away from America. Vietnam is not attacking us. We do not have to defend ourselves. This is a civil war between North and South Vietnam. Each one is trying to control the whole country. We should try to help them make peace, not join their war!

But our government is spending millions of dollars every day to fight this war. More than 500,000 Americans are in Vietnam now, and the government is sending more all the time.

American soldiers in Vietnam

Vietnam War Protesters: How can we stop the war in Vietnam?

(continued)

Comprehension

1. Who are you in this story?

2. How long have U.S. soldiers been fighting in the war in Vietnam?

3. Why did you support the war in the beginning?

4. What is <u>it</u> in the second paragraph?

5. Why have some protesters opposed the war from the beginning?

6. What has changed so that more people now oppose the war?

7. What does <u>this</u> refer to in the fourth paragraph?

8. What is your opinion about the war now?

9. What decision do you have to make?

Decision

● *What should we do to stop the war in Vietnam? Choose one or more of the following options:*

    (a) Oppose the war. Write letters to your representatives and newspapers. Join protests.

    (b) Although you know it is illegal, stop paying your taxes. Let the government put you in jail!

    (c) Do not oppose the war. Maybe the war is wrong, but it is also wrong to oppose the government during a war. The government and the soldiers need your support.

    (d) Support sending more troops and weapons to Vietnam. Tell the government to use nuclear bombs. We cannot win and end the war if we do not fight hard.

    (e) Other: _____

● *Why did you decide that way? Plan how you will explain your decision to your classmates. Write out your reasoning completely.*

President Nixon
Should we bomb the communist Vietnamese camps in Cambodia?

It is February 1969. You are Richard Nixon. Last month you became the President of the United States. Before becoming President, you said that you would bring honor and peace to Vietnam. You said you would do <u>this</u> by negotiating an end to the war and pulling out American troops. There are now more than 500,000 Americans in Vietnam. For nearly 10 years, Americans have been helping and fighting there. Thousands have died. Many Americans are protesting against American involvement. The peace movement in America is getting stronger.

Now the American commanders in Vietnam tell you that they know where the Vietnamese communist headquarters are. <u>They</u> are the most important central military offices of our enemy. They control communist military activities. They are at 15 sites in Cambodia, the country on the western border of Vietnam. The communist North Vietnamese use Cambodia as a safe hiding place. They are in the jungle near Cambodian villages.

The American military commander is asking for permission to bomb the communist headquarters in Cambodia. Cambodia is a neutral country. It is staying out of the war and is not helping either side. The leader of Cambodia, Prince Sihanouk, does not want to help the North Vietnamese or the South Vietnamese. If <u>he</u> helps one side, the other side will be angry with him. He does not want

any fighting to come into Cambodia. He does not want Cambodians to be hurt. He does not want foreigners in Cambodia.

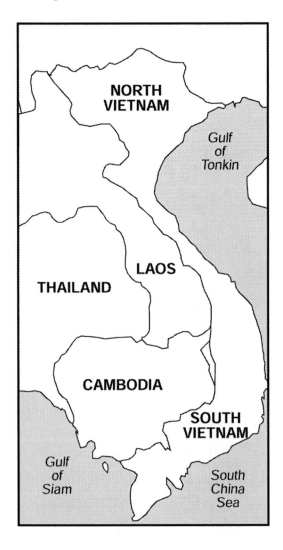

President Nixon: Should we bomb the Communist Vietnamese camps in Cambodia? *(continued)*

Comprehension

1. Who are you in this story?

2. What did you promise the American people?

3. What does <u>this</u> refer to in the first paragraph?

4. Why is it important for us to know where the communist headquarters are?

5. In paragraph 2, who knows where the Vietnamese communist headquarters are?

6. In paragraph 2, what does the word <u>They</u> refer to?

7. Where are the North Vietnamese headquarters?

8. Why are the headquarters there?

9. Who is <u>he</u> in the last paragraph?

10. Why doesn't Prince Sihanouk make the North Vietnamese move the headquarters out of his country?

11. What is a "neutral" country?

12. What are good reasons to bomb the Vietnamese headquarters in Cambodia?

13. What are good reasons not to bomb the Vietnamese headquarters in Cambodia?

14. What decision do you have to make?

Decision

● *Should the U.S. bomb the communist North Vietnamese headquarters in Cambodia? Choose one of the following options:*

   (a) Bomb the headquarters in Cambodia. Keep it a secret. If the press asks about it, lie.
   (b) Bomb the headquarters in Cambodia. Tell Prince Sihanouk and the press about it first.
   (c) Ask Prince Sihanouk for permission to bomb the Vietnamese headquarters.
   (d) Do not attack the communists in Cambodia. It is a neutral country. America has no right carrying the war into a neutral country.
   (e) Try to get Prince Sihanouk to change his mind.
   (f) Attack the headquarters in Cambodia, but do not drop bombs.
   (g) Other: _____

● *Why did you decide that way? Plan how you will explain your decision to your classmates. Write out your reasoning completely.*

Name _____   Date _____

State Legislators
Should we lower the voting age to 18?

It is 1970. You are a member of a state legislature. Should state legislators ratify the Twenty-sixth Amendment to the Constitution to give 18-year-olds the right to vote? The United States is fighting a war in Vietnam. There are thousands of young American soldiers in this war. The government is drafting thousands more. Most of the soldiers are very young—18, 19, and 20 years old. Is it fair to put them in the military? They cannot vote about the war and other important issues, because in America, the voting age is twenty-one. However, many people believe that if a person is old enough to go to war, he is old enough to vote.

What should the national voting age be? When the U.S. became a country, each state made its own laws about who could vote. In all states, only white men could vote. In most states, they had to own property and be at least 21 years old. Since then, the national government has added two amendments about voting to the Constitution. In 1866, the government decided that all male citizens over 21 could vote (Fourteenth Amendment). In 1920, women over 21 got the right to vote (Nineteenth Amendment). If we pass the Twenty-sixth Amendment, all Americans 18 and over can vote in all local, state, and federal elections.

Some people say that 18-year-olds are too young to vote. They will not be responsible enough. Maybe they will vote for foolish things that will be bad for the country.

1776	1866	1920	1971 1976
White male landowners over 21 could vote.	All males over 21 could vote.	All citizens over 21 could vote.	Should 18-year-olds be able to vote?

Name _____ Date _____

Comprehension

1. Who are you in this decision?

2. In paragraph 1, what does the word <u>They</u> refer to?

3. Why can't many American soldiers vote?

4. How have voting rights changed since the U.S. became a country?

5. If the state legislatures ratify this amendment, which elections will 18-year-olds
be able to vote in?

6. For each statement, write *T* for true or *F* for false:

   (a) The government is drafting Americans to fight in Vietnam.

   (b) Black women could vote in 1866.

   (c) This amendment will give the states more control over who can vote.

Decision

- *Should we lower the voting age to 18? Choose one of the following options:*

   (a) No. Leave the voting age at 21.

   (b) Yes. Lower the voting age to 18.

   (c) Change the voting age to _____ years old.

   (d) Other: _____

- *Why did you decide that way? Plan how you will explain your decision to your classmates.
  Write out your reasoning completely.*

Supreme Court Justice
Should capital punishment be legal in the United States?

It is 1971. You are a justice on the Supreme Court. You are listening to arguments about capital punishment, the death penalty. Thirty-nine states allow it for crimes like rape, murder, robbery, kidnapping, treason, and arson. Eleven states do not permit capital punishment for any crime. Before 1967, more than 3,500 criminals were put to death in the U.S. In 1967, you and the other justices stopped capital punishment in the U.S. while you listened to two cases. You now have to decide if the states can continue to use capital punishment. There are now 648 men and women on death row in different states waiting to die. It is hard to make this decision. Listen to the lawyers:

MR. WRIGHT: Violent crime in America is rising! The only way to stop the rising crime rate is to sentence these criminals to death. We must make people know that if they commit a violent crime, they will die.

Electric chair

MR. AMSTERDAM: Capital punishment is wrong. If it is wrong for people to kill, it is wrong for the government to kill. Capital punishment will not scare sick and insane people. People commit these crimes because they are poor and uneducated. Capital punishment will not stop them from being poor and uneducated. In the states that allow capital punishment, who receives the death penalty? It is the poor, the blacks and Indians, the uneducated. This is not fair. And is it fair that Mr. John Doe would be put to death in one state but not another?

MR. WRIGHT: But it is not fair that good, innocent people are murdered and raped, either! And it is not fair that good, innocent people should pay to keep these criminals alive in prisons for the rest of their lives.

MR. AMSTERDAM: Capital punishment is unconstitutional. The Eighth Amendment prohibits cruel and unusual punishment. It is cruel to kill a helpless man or woman. The government must not kill people.

MR. WRIGHT: The men who wrote the Constitution knew about capital punishment. There was capital punishment at that time. If they thought capital punishment was "cruel and unusual punishment," why didn't they write that in the Eighth Amendment?

The nine justices must now decide if capital punishment is constitutional or unconstitutional. If it is unconstitutional, it is illegal.

Supreme Court Justice: Should capital punishment be legal in the United States? *(continued)*

Comprehension

1. Who are you?

2. What do you have to decide about?

3. Is the death penalty legal now?

4. Has the death penalty ever been legal?

5. Why are people on death row?

6. What does Mr. Amsterdam mean by <u>It</u> in the third paragraph?

7. Who is Mr. John Doe?

8. What does Mr. Wright mean by <u>that time</u> in the sixth paragraph?

9. What does <u>they</u> refer to in the sixth paragraph?

10. For each statement, write *F* for fact or O for opinion. Remember that facts are things that can be checked and agreed to by everyone. Opinions are a person's own ideas.

    (a) Violent crime is increasing.
    (b) The death penalty will stop people from committing violent crimes.
    (c) All the states allow capital punishment now.
    (d) Capital punishment laws are not the same in different states.
    (e) Capital punishment laws should be the same in all states.
    (f) The Constitution says that capital punishment is all right.
    (g) The Constitution says that capital punishment is not all right.
    (h) People commit crimes because they are poor and uneducated.

Decision

- *What should the Supreme Court say about capital punishment? Choose one of the following options:*

    (a) Vote that each state may decide whether or not capital punishment is legal.
    (b) Vote that capital punishment is illegal in all states because it is not given equally to men and women and all races.
    (c) Vote that capital punishment is illegal in all states because it is unconstitutional.
    (d) Vote that capital punishment is constitutional and legal in all the United States.

    (e) Other: _____

- *Why did you decide that way? Plan how you will explain your decision to your classmates. Write out your reasoning completely.*

Supreme Court Justice
Should abortion be legal?

1973

It is 1973, and you are a justice on the Supreme Court. The issue is abortion. Should pregnant women who do not want to have a baby be able to end the pregnancy? Four states allow women to have abortions for any reason if they have them early in their pregnancy. However, 31 states have laws that make abortions legal only if the mother's health is in danger. Women are challenging the laws in two of these states, Texas and Georgia. You are listening to lawyers present cases about these two states' laws. There are two questions. First, does a woman have the right to an abortion? Second, does a state have the right to limit abortions?

MS. WEDDINGTON: It is a woman's right to decide whether or not to have a baby. It is her body. If she does not want to have the baby, the state should not force her to have it. There are many reasons not to have a baby. Her health is only one reason. If she was raped or if a family member made her pregnant, should she have to have the baby? If she cannot take care of the baby, should the law force her to have it? These are private decisions. Only the woman can make these decisions. The Constitution protects people's rights to privacy. Abortion is a private decision.

However, the Texas and Georgia laws make too many abortions illegal. In these states, doctors and hospitals cannot help many women who want abortions. Rich women can travel to other countries or states to have abortions. But poor women in these states cannot afford that. They have abortions, but not in clean hospitals. They often get infections from dirty, dangerous abortions, and many poor women die. All women must have the right to safe, clean abortions.

MR. FLOYD: When a woman decides to have an abortion, she is making a decision for the baby, too. She is deciding to kill a living baby! That baby has fingers and toes and a beating heart! But can the baby protect itself? Can the baby speak out? Doesn't the baby have a right to live? Who is going to speak for the baby? The state must protect the baby. A baby is protected by the law even before it is born. Murder is illegal. A mother does not have the right to kill a baby at any time.

SUPREME COURT JUSTICE: When does the law begin to protect an unborn fetus?

MR. FLOYD: We believe that the law protects it from the time it begins to have life.

JUSTICE: When is that?

MR. FLOYD: Nobody knows for sure. We believe it begins about seven days after conception.

MS. WEDDINGTON: We believe that the Constitution protects people after they are born, not before.

1800	1828	1967	1970
Common law accepted abortions if before fetus moves around.	New York passed first law making abortion illegal except to save mother's life.	States began changing anti-abortion laws because abortions were safer than before.	31 states prohibited abortion except to save mother's life; 15 allow it for various reasons; 4 permit it for any reason.

Name _____ Date _____

Supreme Court Justice: Should abortion be legal? *(continued)*

Comprehension ◥◕◔◭◕◔◭◕◔◭◕◔

1. Who are you in this decision?
2. What do you have to decide?
3. What is an abortion?
4. Do any states allow abortions now?
5. Is Ms. Weddington arguing for or against legalized abortion?
6. Is Mr. Floyd arguing for or against legalizing abortion?
7. Which of the following arguments are *against* legalizing abortion?
    (a) Sometimes a woman doesn't want to have a baby.
    (b) The Constitution protects people after they are born, not before.
    (c) Fetuses have rights, too.
    (d) Abortion is a private decision that only a woman can make.
    (e) The Constitution protects all life, even before it is born.
    (f) Life begins before birth.
    (g) Poor people can't get abortions in some states, but rich women can go to other places to get them.
    (h) Women who want abortions will have them even if they are unsafe.
    (i) The Constitution must protect even unborn babies.
    (j) A fetus cannot live on its own before it is seven months old.
    (k) Even a fetus has fingers, toes, and a beating heart.

Decision ◥◕◔◭◕◔◭◕◔◭◕◔

● *Should women have the right to abortions? Can Texas and Georgia restrict abortions? Choose one of the following options:*

    (a) Vote that each state has the right to make laws about abortion. The Supreme Court has no right to decide about a state's abortion laws.
    (b) Vote that the two states' laws are against the U.S. Constitution. Women have the right to abortions any time for any reason.
    (c) Vote that the two states' laws are unfair. Women must be able to have abortions under certain conditions:

        1. _____

        2. _____

        3. _____

    (d) Vote that women do not have the right to an abortion. The Constitution says nothing about abortions or privacy.
    (e) Other: _____

● *Why did you decide that way? Plan how you will explain your decision to your classmates. Write out your reasoning completely.*

U.S. Congress

1974

Is the president of the United States above the law?

It is July 1974. You are a congressperson in the House of Representatives in Washington, D.C. This is a very serious problem for you to decide: Should you vote to impeach President Nixon?

Two years ago, five men broke into the Watergate office building in Washington, D.C. Police caught them stealing papers from the office of the Democratic National Committee. The FBI began to investigate. It discovered that the burglars were working for the Republican Committee to Reelect the President. Immediately, President Nixon said that he and his staff knew nothing about the burglary. In November 1972, he was reelected.

Two months later, the burglars were found guilty in court. The Senate appointed a committee to find out who had sent these men to steal the papers. Did President Nixon have anything to do with it? A House committee also started investigating.

During the next year and a half, the court and the committees uncovered new information. They learned that one of President Nixon's closest friends was the boss of the burglary. The burglars had been paid thousands of dollars not to talk. Some of them admitted that they had lied in court. Some of them said that the president's top advisers were helping to cover up the truth.

In July, they learned that President Nixon had made tapes of all his conversations in the White House. When the judge asked for the tapes,

the president refused to give them to him. He said that a president is above the law and has special privileges. For a year, the court and the Senate committee tried to force the president to give them the tapes, but he would not. Finally, the Supreme Court decided that he had to give the tapes to the judge. When the president gave him the tapes, two were missing, and many minutes had been erased. What was on the missing tapes? What was erased? Who lost and erased them, and why?

What did the tapes say? On one tape, only six days after the burglary, President Nixon told the FBI to stop the investigation. That proves that he was trying to hide the truth.

Now your committee has to decide what to do next. If the president did something illegal, you can vote to impeach him. That means he will be on trial in the Senate. The Senate can decide to remove him from office. No president has ever been removed from office. President Nixon could be the first! What if the president goes to jail? What will this do to the U.S.? An American president has never gone to jail! What will other countries think about the U.S.? Many Americans like President Nixon very much. They think he has been a very good president. Many people think the burglary was not very important. They think the president made only a little, unimportant mistake. But is a president above the law? Is it all right for a president to lie to the people? Is it all right for a president to try to hide the truth?

U.S. Congress: Is the president of the U.S. above the law? *(continued)*

Comprehension

1. What do you have to decide?

2. If you vote to impeach, what will happen to the president?

3. Why do you think the burglars were stealing papers?

4. Who told the men to steal the papers?

5. Who paid the burglars not to talk in court?

6. What were they paid not to talk about?

7. Who had made tapes?

8. What was on the tapes?

9. Why were the tapes important?

10. Why didn't President Nixon think he had to give the tapes to the judge?

11. Why do you think he didn't want to give the tapes to the judge?

12. Who forced him to turn over the tapes to the judge?

13. What was wrong with the tapes?

14. Who do you think did that to the tapes?

15. What did the tapes prove?

16. How did the tapes prove that President Nixon was guilty of something?

17. What was President Nixon guilty of doing?

18. Who will decide if President Nixon should be impeached?

1974   **U.S. Congress: Is the president of the U.S. above the law?** *(continued)*

19. Put these events in the order in which they occurred. Number them from 1 to 12.

____ President Nixon said he was not involved in the burglary.

____ President Nixon recorded his conversations.

____ President Nixon was reelected.

____ The judge asked President Nixon to give him the tapes.

____ The Supreme Court decided that he had to give the tapes to the judge.

____ Five men tried to steal papers from the Democratic National Committee.

____ The President's aide said that there were tapes of the President's conversations.

____ One of the burglars said that Nixon's friend was the boss.

____ The president refused to give the tapes to the judge.

____ The president gave the tapes to the judge, but some were missing and erased.

____ The tapes proved that Nixon was trying to cover up the truth.

____ President Nixon told the FBI to stop the investigation.

Decision

- *Should the House committee vote to impeach President Nixon? Choose one of the following options:*

    (a) Vote to impeach President Nixon.

    (b) Vote not to impeach President Nixon.

    (c) Other: _____

- *Why did you decide that way? Plan how you will explain your decision to your classmates. Write out your reasoning completely.*

Name _____ Date _____

1974

President Ford
Should you pardon Richard Nixon?

It is September 1974. You are Gerald Ford, thirty-eighth president of the U.S. You have an important decision to make about Richard Nixon, the thirty-seventh president.

President Gerald Ford

One month ago, Richard Nixon resigned as president. No other president has ever resigned. Nixon resigned when he realized that Congress would probably impeach him. Congress said that he was trying to block justice. Nixon knew about the 1972 Watergate burglary, but he tried to cover it up. He tried to stop the investigation. He did not tell the whole truth. He did not obey the courts. Nixon said that a president has special privileges that make him above the law. Congress and the courts said the opposite—Nixon was using the power of the presidency wrongly.

You had been Nixon's vice president. When Mr. Nixon resigned, you became the president one month ago. Mr. Nixon could still be tried in court. It is even possible that he could be put in jail. No president has ever been put in jail. What will trying a former president do to the country? How will Americans feel if he is found guilty and goes to jail? How will they feel if he is *not* found guilty and does *not* go to jail? What will foreign countries think? Americans are very divided about Mr. Nixon. Some say he is a criminal and should go to jail. Others say he was a great president who just made some mistakes. Most people agree on one thing: This scandal should be resolved as soon as possible.

What are your options? If you do nothing, Nixon could go to jail. You could order the Justice Department to sue him in court, or *not* to sue him. You could also pardon Mr. Nixon. This means no one could sue him for his part in the Watergate scandal while he was president.

1974   ## President Ford: Should you pardon Richard Nixon? *(continued)*

Comprehension

1. Who are you in this story?

2. How did you become the president of the U.S.?

3. How long have you been president?

4. Why isn't Richard Nixon the president now?

5. What did Nixon try to cover up?

6. What do some people think he is guilty of doing?

7. Why might Mr. Nixon go to jail?

8. What are some reasons why he should go to jail?

9. What are some reasons why he should not go to jail?

10. What will happen if Mr. Nixon goes to court?

Decision

● *What should you do? Choose one of the following options:*

   (a) Do nothing. Let the courts and the Justice Department decide what to do.

   (b) Tell the Justice Department not to sue Mr. Nixon in court.

   (c) Tell the Justice Department to sue Mr. Nixon in court.

   (d) Pardon Mr. Nixon.

   (e) Other: _____

● *Why did you decide that way? Plan how you will explain your decision to your classmates. Write out your reasoning completely.*

Supreme Court

1974

What rights do non-English-speaking students have?

It is 1974. You are a justice of the United States Supreme Court. The Court is listening to arguments about education. Should public schools have to teach in languages other than English?

Chinese parents in San Francisco, California, are asking the Court to make the public schools give special classes to children who do not speak English. The San Francisco public schools say that it is not their responsibility to provide special classes for students who cannot speak English. Listen to their arguments.

PARENTS: We are new in this country. We know that our children need to study hard and get a good education in order to be successful in America. There are many Chinese children in San Francisco schools who cannot speak English. They are learning it, but learning a new language takes time. Our children are falling behind in math, history, science, and other subjects because their English is not good enough yet. We want the schools to teach these classes in our language. That way, our children can learn as much as the American students are learning.

SAN FRANCISCO SCHOOL DISTRICT: Our schools have many different kinds of students—rich and poor, fast learners and slow learners, English-speaking students and non-English-speaking students. We want to help all students learn,

but we should teach our classes only in English. If we have special classes just for Chinese students, we will have to buy Chinese language books and hire teachers who can teach in Chinese. What if the Mexican and Filipino parents want native language classes for their children? We cannot teach in all these languages! California law says that English should be the language of teaching for all schools. We agree. The Court should not force us to teach in other languages.

Supreme Court: What rights do non-English-speaking students have? *(continued)*

Comprehension

1. Who are you in this decision?
2. What do the Chinese parents want?
3. Why do they want this?
4. What does the San Francisco School District want?
5. Why do they want this?
6. According to the reading, what other languages do students speak in San Francisco schools?
7. For each statement, write *T* for true or *F* for false:
   (a) The Chinese parents do not want their children to learn English.
   (b) California already has a law about the language of teaching.
   (c) The Chinese parents want all children in the schools to learn Chinese.
   (d) Special classes for Chinese children will require new books and new teachers.
8. For each statement, write *F* for fact or O for opinion. Remember that facts are things that can be checked. Opinions are a person's own ideas.
   (a) There are many kinds of students in San Francisco schools.
   (b) It takes time to learn a new language.
   (c) All Americans should speak English.

Decision

- *What rights should non-English-speaking students have? Choose one or more of the following options:*
   (a) Let each state make its own decision on this question.
   (b) Schools must do something to help students who do not speak English well, but they can decide the best way to do this.
   (c) Schools must teach classes in the languages of all their students.
   (d) Schools must teach classes in the languages of all groups with more than _____ students.
   (e) English should be the only language of public schools, but there should be special classes in which the teacher is trained to teach English as a Second Language.
   (f) All students should be in mainstream English classes. There should be no special classes for students who do not know English.
   (g) Other: _____

- *Why did you decide that way? Plan how you will explain your decision to your classmates. Write out your reasoning completely.*

▽ 1979 ▽

American Citizens
What should we do to get our hostages out of Iran?

Ayatollah Khomeini

It is November 1979. You are an American, and you are angry, worried, and confused. A few days ago, you and all America watched a terrible event happen on television. A mob of militant revolutionaries in Iran took over the American Embassy in Tehran, the capital. They kidnapped 66 Americans who were working there. They put blindfolds on them and locked them up. They shouted bad things about America. The Embassy represents the U.S. in Iran. The government of Iran was supposed to protect the people who work for the embassy. However, Iran's government seems to be supporting the militants. Why?

For more than 20 years, the U.S. has supported the Shah of Iran. He was trying to modernize his country by bringing American culture to Iran. He opposed communism, and he let the U.S. have military bases in Iran. Under the Shah, Iran was a good friend of America.

However, many Iranians did not like the Shah. They said he was a cruel dictator. They believed that he was turning away from the Moslem religious beliefs. They did not want to be like the United States. They wanted a religious society and a religious government. Finally, the people of Iran overthrew the Shah

in January 1979. They supported Ayatollah Khomeini, a religious leader. The Shah fled from Iran and came to the U.S. He has cancer and needs medical attention.

The militants say the U.S. is the cause of all Iran's problems. They say the Shah is a criminal. They say he stole from the people of Iran. They say the Shah used to imprison, torture, and kill Iranians who disagreed with him. They say the U.S. helped him do these things. They want the U.S. to send him back to Iran for a trial. They kidnapped the American Embassy workers to force the U.S. to return the Shah. They say that some of the Embassy workers were spies. Maybe they will kill or torture the hostages.

All Americans want these hostages freed. They should immediately be sent home safely. What can America do?

Shah of Iran as a young man

American Citizens: What should we do to get our hostages out of Iran (continued)

Comprehension

1. Who are you in this story?
2. What are Americans upset about?
3. Who put blindfolds on people?
4. Whom did they put the blindfolds on?
5. What do the Iranians want?
6. Who does not like the Shah?
7. Who is the Shah of Iran?
8. Why does the U.S. like the Shah?
9. In the fourth paragraph, who are <u>They</u>?
10. In the fourth paragraph, what do <u>these things</u> refer to?
11. Why are the Iranian revolutionaries angry at the U.S.?
12. Why are the Iranian revolutionaries angry at their Shah?
13. Why did the revolutionaries kidnap American Embassy workers?

Decision

● *What should the U.S. do to get American hostages back? Choose one or more*
  of the following options:

   (a) Send the Shah back to Iran. We want our Americans back safely.
   (b) Don't send the Shah back to Iran. He was our good friend, and we
       must protect him now.
   (c) Send a military force to invade Iran and rescue the hostages.
   (d) Ask the United Nations to punish Iran economically. All the countries
       should stop selling things to Iran and stop buying things from Iran
       Then the country will be hurt and will release the hostages.
   (e) Kidnap the Iranian Embassy workers in the U.S.
   (f) Send all Iranian students who are studying in the U.S. back to Iran.
   (g) Apologize to Iran for supporting the Shah. Try to make peace with
       the militants and the Iranian government.
   (h) Wait. Let's see what happens. Don't do anything.
   (i) Ask the Shah to go to another country.
   (j) Take all the money that the Iranian government has in American banks.
       When the hostages are released, we will return this money to Iran.
   (k) Other: _____

● *Why did you decide that way? Plan how you will explain your decision to your classmates.*
  Write out your reasoning completely.

1979

American Citizens
Should we continue to develop nuclear power?

It is March 1979. You are an American citizen. There has just been an accident at the Three Mile Island nuclear power plant in Pennsylvania. A valve broke inside the plant, but the workers did not think the problem was serious. They did not do anything to fix the problem, and it got much worse. Inside the plant, there were millions of gallons of radioactive water and steam. Thousands of people evacuated the towns around the plant because they were afraid that it would explode. It was difficult to leave the area because there was no evacuation plan. The plant did not explode, and nobody was hurt. The plant is still shut down. The government and the plant's owners are still studying what happened at Three Mile Island.

Your state has a nuclear power plant very similar to the one at Three Mile Island. They were built around the same time and have the same design. One more plant is in construction and there are plans to build others. Your state gets 20 percent of its electricity from nuclear power. When the new plants are ready, it will be 50 percent. More plants will make more nuclear waste. This is the radioactive garbage that remains after electricity is produced. If it gets into the air, soil, or water, it can hurt and even kill animals and people. Nuclear waste lasts for a very long time, so it must be stored in a very safe place. We have temporary sites for the radioactive waste but no permanent site. In the future, we will need

to build a permanent place to store the waste, or pay another state to store it for us.

Some people want to pass a law against nuclear power in our state. This is what your neighbors are saying.

IN FAVOR OF NUCLEAR POWER: We should not depend on foreign countries for our oil, as we used to. With nuclear power, someday we will produce all the energy we need right here in America. We can produce it cheaply, too. Everybody wants low electric bills. Besides, there has never been an explosion at a nuclear power plant. The new plants are safe and we can make them even safer. We should continue to develop nuclear power.

AGAINST NUCLEAR POWER: The problem at Three Mile Island proves that nuclear power is not safe. There was almost a terrible disaster. Thousands of people could have been hurt or killed by radiation from the plant. They couldn't even drive away from it because of the traffic jams! And there is no good way to store the wastes from nuclear plants. This poisonous material lasts for hundreds of thousands of years! We do not want it in our state. If we pay another state to store the waste, then the price of nuclear power will increase. Nuclear power is not good for our state.

American Citizens: Should we continue to develop nuclear power?
(continued)

Comprehension ≈◦◡◭◦◡◭◦◡◭◦◡≈

1. Who are you in this decision?

2. What happened at Three Mile Island?

3. Why is the accident in Pennsylvania important to our state?

4. In paragraph 2, what does the word <u>They</u> refer to?

5. What is nuclear waste? Where does it come from?

6. What is dangerous for people if we breathe or drink it?

7. What are three arguments in favor of nuclear power?

8. What are three arguments against nuclear power?

Decision ≈◦◡◭◦◡◭◦◡◭◦◡≈

- *What should our state do about nuclear power? Choose one or more of the following options:*

    (a) Shut down the plant we already have.

    (b) Stop building the plant under construction.

    (c) Cancel the orders for the new plants.

    (d) Build only the plants we have plans for.

    (e) Plan and build more nuclear power plants.

    (f) Build a permanent waste site in our state.

    (g) Pay another state or country to take our nuclear waste.

    (h) Transport our nuclear waste to the ocean and dump it.

    (i) Pay for more research on nuclear power.

    (j) Look for other ways to make electricity.

    (k) Other: _____

- *Why did you decide that way? Plan how you will explain your decision to your classmates. Write out your reasoning completely.*

American Citizens
What should we do about the Southeast Asian refugees?

It is 1980. You are an American citizen. During the past year, hundreds of thousands of people have been leaving their countries in Southeast Asia. Laotians, Cambodians, and Vietnamese have been going to Hong Kong, Malaysia, Thailand, Indonesia, and the Philippines. They want to settle in other countries such as the U.S., China, Australia, Canada, and France. Many of them say they would have been killed if they had stayed in their countries. They are fleeing violence and imprisonment.

When the U.S. secretly dropped bombs in Cambodia during the Vietnam War, many Cambodians stopped supporting the Cambodian government. There was a civil war, which a communist group called the Khmer Rouge won five years ago. Since then, the Khmer Rouge communists have murdered more than one million Cambodians.

In Laos in the 1960's and 1970's, communists from North Vietnam and China were supporting communist Laotians. The U.S. supported Laotians who were against communism. The communists won in 1975 and took control of the country. Some Laotians are still fighting against the communist army. The communist government imprisons and kills these people.

In Vietnam, there was a war between the communists in the North and the anticommunists in the South. The U.S. helped South Vietnam, and the war continued until 1975.

More than one million Vietnamese were killed. North Vietnam won the war and took over the government for the whole country. Now, the new government is killing and imprisoning the people who were friendly to the U.S.

Some of the refugees are afraid they will be killed or punished in their own countries. They are called political refugees. Others say they cannot have a good life in their countries because of communism. They want to move to other countries where they can have their own businesses. They are called economic refugees.

The United Nations has started refugee camps to help the refugees. There are schools and health clinics in the camps. However, Thailand and the other countries do not want these refugees to stay there for a long time. They want them to settle quickly in other countries. Some countries, such as Japan, will not accept refugees. Australia will accept them if they have skills or education or family members already there. Other countries will accept refugees if they have good reasons to leave their countries. What should the U.S. do about the Southeast Asian refugees?

© 1997 J. Weston Walch, Publisher

1980

American Citizens: What should we do about the
Southeast Asian refugees? *(continued)*

Comprehension

1. What countries are the refugees leaving from now?

2. What countries are they going to?

3. Why are they leaving their countries?

4. In Paragraph 5 who are the <u>Others</u>?

5. What is the difference between political and economic refugees?

6. What countries do the refugees want to settle in?

7. In Paragraph 6, who are <u>They</u>?

8. Why do you think that Thailand, Indonesia, Hong Kong, and the Philippines want the refugees to leave quickly?

9. Why do you think some countries do not want to accept refugees?

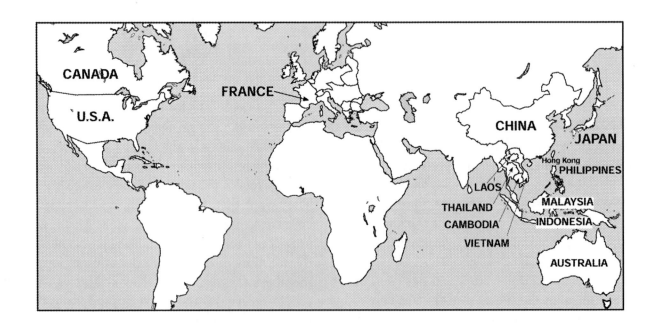

Name _____ Date _____

American Citizens: What should we do about the Southeast Asian refugees? *(continued)*

Decision

- *What should the U.S. do about the Southeast Asian refugees? Choose one or more of the following options:*

    (a) Accept all refugees who apply to come to the United States. America is the land of freedom. We have always welcomed refugees and immigrants here. All Americans are immigrants.

    (b) Accept all refugees from these countries. These people were friends of the U.S. during the wars in their countries. Now we must help them.

    (c) Accept only political refugees. Do not accept economic refugees. They just want a better life.

    (d) Put a quota on the number of refugees we will accept in a year. We cannot take all of them at one time. That will be too hard for America. We should accept only (number) each year.

    (e) Accept only the educated refugees. They will be able to help America. The uneducated refugees will be a lot of trouble for America. They will not be able to get jobs.

    (f) Accept the uneducated refugees. They will take the jobs that Americans do not want to do. They will work for low pay.

    (g) Do not accept any refugees. They will not be happy here. America is very different from their countries. It is better for them to return to their own countries after the fighting has stopped.

    (h) Do not accept any refugees. They cannot solve the problems in their countries if they come here. If they really believe in freedom and democracy, they should return to their countries to help solve the problems.

    (i) Do not accept any refugees. The U.S. already has too many problems. We have many poor and homeless and unemployed people here already. We cannot take care of more people.

    (j) Ask other countries to take more refugees.

    (k) Other: _____

- *Why did you decide that way? Plan how you will explain your decision to your classmates. Write out your reasoning completely.*

American Citizens

1982

Should we approve the Equal Rights Amendment?

It is 1982. You are an American citizen. Your state legislature is discussing an amendment to the U.S. Constitution. It is called the Equal Rights Amendment, or ERA. To amend the Constitution, both the Senate and the House of Representatives must approve. Then 38 of the 50 state legislatures must approve. The House approved the ERA in 1971, and the Senate approved it in 1972. Thirty-five states have also approved the ERA. Now your state legislature is debating it.

The Equal Rights Amendment guarantees that men and women have equal rights. Many people are in favor of this amendment. They say that the Constitution does not guarantee equal rights to women. Because of that, there is a lot of discrimination against women.

Some discrimination is in jobs. For example, why are so few women lawyers, doctors, engineers, bus drivers, police officers, and businesspeople? One reason is that many colleges have not accepted women to study for some of these professions. Another reason is that some companies do not want to hire women for certain jobs.

Another kind of job discrimination is in salaries and promotions. Women receive lower salaries than men even though they do the same work. There are laws against that, such as the 1963 Equal Pay Act, but women still get much lower salaries for doing the same work. Also, very few women are promoted to be managers or bosses.

There are other kinds of discrimination, too. For example, a husband has more rights than his wife. A woman's husband owns the property and money. In some places, it is hard for a woman to borrow money from a bank without her husband's permission. Some banks make it hard for a woman to have a bank account in her own name.

There are laws that should stop discrimination, but they are not just for women. The ERA will make it easy to stop these kinds of discrimination against women. If the ERA passes, the Constitution will make sexual discrimination illegal.

However, there are many people who are against the ERA. They say that men and women are different and should not be treated the same. There are some jobs that women cannot do. For example, women should not have to fight in the military. If the ERA passes, maybe women will be drafted into the military. Maybe an employer will force women to do the same heavy work as men do. Also, women have special privileges now which they will lose if the ERA passes. When a husband and wife divorce, will the woman still be able to receive alimony from her ex-husband? Will a husband who abandons his family still have to pay child support? Will the ERA make it hard for women to stay home and take care of their children? If men and women are equal, who will take care of the children? Who will work outside the home?

(continued)

1982

American Citizens: Should we approve the
Equal Rights Amendment? *(continued)*

Finally, some people say we do not need the ERA. The Constitution already protects women under the Fifth and Fourteenth Amendments. Women can already use the Constitution to fight against discrimination in court. The 1963 Equal Pay Act and the 1964 Civil Rights Act already protect women against discrimination. We do not need more laws. We just need to enforce the laws we have.

There are good arguments for and against the ERA. The ERA raises many questions. How do you want your state legislators to vote?

ERA supporters

Name _____ Date _____

American Citizens: Should we approve the
Equal Rights Amendment? *(continued)*

Comprehension

1. Who are you in this story?

2. List three examples of gender discrimination in employment.

3. List one kind of gender discrimination in education.

4. Why isn't it fair for a husband to own the property and money?

5. Why isn't it fair for a woman to need her husband's permission to borrow money?

6. In the second paragraph, what does the word <u>that</u> refer to?

7. What protections might women lose if the ERA passes?

8. What privileges might women lose if the ERA passes?

9. Why do some people say that we do not need the ERA to stop gender discrimination?

10. How many more states need to approve the ERA before it becomes an amendment?

11. For each statement, write *F* for fact or *O* for opinion. Remember that facts are things that can be checked and agreed to by everyone. Opinions are a person's own ideas.

    (a) Thirty-five states have approved the ERA.
    (b) Both the Senate and the House have to approve an amendment.
    (c) There is discrimination against women.
    (d) Women can do many jobs that men can do.
    (e) Women should be able to serve in the military.
    (f) Women receive lower salaries than men.
    (g) A woman must have her husband's permission to borrow money.
    (h) Men and women are different.
    (i) Women need special protection.
    (j) Women will lose their special protection if the ERA passes.

Decision

● *How do you want your state legislature to vote? Choose one of the following options:*

    (a) Vote in favor of the Equal Rights Amendment.
    (b) Vote against the Equal Rights Amendment.
    (c) Other: _____

● *Why did you decide that way? Plan how you will explain your decision to your classmates. Write out your reasoning completely.*

American Citizens

1986

How can we stop the use of illegal drugs?

It is 1986. You are an American citizen. You are very concerned about the use of drugs in America. Both adults and young people are using illegal drugs. These drugs are dangerous, and many people die from using them. AIDS is spreading among people who share infected needles. The drugs are also expensive, and addicts commit crimes to get money to buy them. America is becoming sick, violent, and unsafe. We must do something about illegal drugs.

Some people say that we should spend more money to fight drug use. We need more police to stop the sale of drugs, and we need to stop drugs from coming into America from other countries. We could use the military to stop drugs at our borders, and we could tell other countries to stop producing drugs.

Inside America, we could make stronger punishments for people who use and sell drugs, but if we do this we might need more prisons. We could also start programs to teach young people that drugs are dangerous.

Other people say that we will never be able to stop people from buying and using drugs. It is almost impossible to stop drugs from entering America. But if we legalize drugs, the prices will go down. Then there will not be so much violence and crime, because drug users will be able to afford their drugs. Also, the government could tax the sale of the drugs and use the money to educate young people about the dangers of drugs.

What do you want your state and national representatives to do about the drug problem?

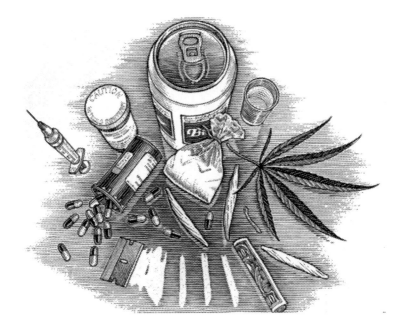

American Citizens: How can we stop the use of illegal drugs?
(continued)

Comprehension

1. Who are you in this decision?

2. How do some addicts get money to buy drugs?

3. How do drugs hurt America?

4. What places do you think illegal drugs come from?

5. What are some ways to stop the use of illegal drugs?

6. Why do you think more prisons might be needed?

7. How could legalizing drugs help America?

8. What are reasons not to legalize drugs?

Decision

- *What can we do to stop the use of illegal drugs in America? Choose one or more of the following options:*

  (a) Educate people about the danger of drugs.
  (b) Establish drug-counseling programs to help people who want
       to stop using drugs.
  (c) Increase the penalty for using illegal drugs.
  (d) Increase the penalty for selling drugs.
  (e) Hire more police.
  (f) Try to catch and punish more drug users.
  (g) Try to catch and punish more drug dealers.
  (h) Build more prisons.
  (i) Make drugs legal.
  (j) Help drug-producing nations fight against drug cultivation.
  (k) Use the military to stop drugs from entering the U.S.
  (l) Stop being friendly to any governments and politicians involved in drug dealing.
  (m) Ask the United Nations to do something about the cultivation of illegal drugs.
  (n) Make American workers pass drug tests.
  (o) Other: _____

- *Why did you decide that way? Plan how you will explain your decision to your classmates.*
  Write out your reasoning completely.

1987

U.S. Congress
What should we do about the Iran-Contra scandal?

It is 1987. You are a U.S. congressperson. You have just learned that government employees have lied to Congress about U.S. activities in Nicaragua. These government workers say that President Reagan and his advisers told them to break the law. Now you are deciding what to do.

President Reagan does not like the Nicaraguan government. He says that it is a communist government. He supports the Contras, a group of rebels fighting against the Nicaraguan government. He convinced Congress to send over $100 million to the Contras. In 1982, Congress passed the Boland Amendment, which said that the CIA and other government agencies could not help the Contras anymore. However, some people in the government disagreed with this policy. They still wanted to send money to the Contras, even if it was against the law. They found different ways to raise money for the Contras. First, they convinced some rich governments to give money to the Contras. This was not illegal, but they did not tell the American people about it. Then they allowed Israel to sell U.S. weapons to Iran without telling us. That was illegal. Besides, Iran has been our enemy for about 10 years. Later, the administration itself even sold missiles to Iran!

The U.S. government used the profits from the weapon sales to buy and deliver supplies to the Contras. Once, the Nicaraguan government shot down a Contra supply plane. The only survivor was an American

man who said that the plane was owned by the CIA. This meant that the American CIA was illegally sending supplies to the Contras.

Some people say that the Colombian drug cartels also delivered supplies to the Contras. The U.S. government paid for this help by allowing them to fly Colombian cocaine into the United States.

Reagan's aides were selling weapons to our enemies, and maybe even helping drugs come into America, in order to support the Contras in Nicaragua. They say that they were doing what President Reagan wanted them to do. Some of them say that Reagan did not know about these illegal activities. They say that they did not tell the President what they were doing because they wanted to protect him. President Reagan says that he did not know about the illegal support for the Contras. Some Americans say he is not telling the truth.

Name _____ Date _____

U.S. Congress: What should we do about the Iran-Contra scandal?
(continued)

Comprehension ∾◦◿◦◿◦◿◦◿

1. Who are you in this decision?

2. Why does President Reagan support the Contras?

3. What does the Boland Amendment say?

4. In paragraph 2, what do the words <u>this policy</u> refer to?

5. In paragraph 2, what does the word <u>That</u> refer to?

6. How did some government workers help the Contras after Congress passed the Boland Amendment?

7. How did Reagan's aides break the law?

8. Do you think it is important for a president to know what his/her advisers are doing?

9. For each statement, write *F* for fact or *O* for opinion. Remember that facts are things that can be checked and agreed to by everyone. Opinions are a person's own ideas.

    (a) The American government broke the law by supporting the Contras.
    (b) President Reagan told his aides to continue supporting the Contras even after the Boland Amendment.
    (c) Transporting cocaine into the U.S. is illegal.

Decision ∾◦◿◦◿◦◿◦◿

- *What should we do about the Iran-Contra scandal? Choose one or more of the following options:*

    (a) Nothing. The president has the power to make foreign policy decisions.
    (b) Nothing. However, we should have a trial and put his aides in jail if they broke the law.
    (c) Make a new, stronger law to stop the Reagan administration from helping the Contras.
    (d) Impeach the president.
    (e) Appoint a panel to investigate whether the president knew about illegal support for the Contras.
    (f) Other: _____

- *Why did you decide that way? Plan how you will explain your decision to your classmates. Write out your reasoning completely.*

Name _____ Date _____

American Citizens
What should we do about Iraq?

It is August 1990. You are an American citizen. In the Middle East, Iraq has just invaded her small neighbor Kuwait. The royal family of Kuwait has escaped to Saudi Arabia, but a thousand Kuwaitis have been killed. Iraq has a large and powerful military. Iraqi soldiers are experienced fighters. They have modern weapons that they bought from the U.S.

Why is Iraq invading Kuwait? Iraq's leader, Saddam Hussein, says that Kuwait used to be a part of Iraq and still should belong to Iraq. Hussein says that Kuwait has disobeyed oil-producing rules. He says that Kuwait has been producing more oil than it is supposed to. This lowers the price of oil and hurts all oil-producing countries. He also says Kuwait has been stealing Iraqi oil. Finally, he

believes that Kuwait is too friendly with the U.S. and Israel. Kuwait is Arab and must work together with the Arabs.

The American government believes that Hussein wants to control Kuwait and the oil that is there. Iraq has just ended a 10-year war with Iran, and it needs billions of dollars to pay its debts. Kuwait has very rich oil fields that could help pay the debts. Hussein wants to keep the price of oil high. He wants to become the leader of the Arab oil-producing countries.

Kuwait is an ally of the U.S. The U.S. opposes one country invading and taking over another country. We also want peace in the Middle East because we need oil from this region, including Kuwait.

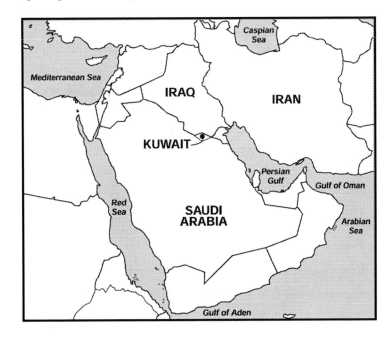

1990

American Citizens: What should we do about Iraq? *(continued)*

Comprehension

1. Who are you in this story?

2. For each statement, write *T* for true, *F* for false, or *N* for not given.

  (a) Iraq's army attacked Kuwait.
  (b) Many Iraqis were killed in the attack.
  (c) Saddam Hussein is the king of Kuwait.
  (d) Hussein wants to control Kuwait's oil.
  (e) Hussein needs money to pay debts to Iran.
  (f) Iraq wants the price of oil to be high.
  (g) Hussein says that Kuwait has been selling oil cheap.
  (h) Hussein says that Kuwait has been selling Iraq's oil.
  (i) The U.S. believes that Hussein wants to lead the Arab oil-producing countries.
  (j) The U.S. is a friend of Kuwait.
  (k) The U.S. doesn't want to pay high prices for oil.

3. What does <u>This</u> refer to in the second paragraph?

4. What does <u>it</u> refer to in the third paragraph?

5. What are three reasons that the U.S. is upset with Saddam Hussein?

Decision

● *What should the U.S. do? Choose one or more of the following options:*

  (a) Send American troops to defend Kuwait. Push Iraq's army back to Iraq.
  (b) Send American troops to defeat Iraq. Continue fighting until
      Saddam Hussein is captured or killed.
  (c) Send American troops to protect Saudi Arabia. Kuwait is next to
      Saudi Arabia, and Iraq might try to take over the Saudi oil fields.
      Saudi Arabia is our ally, and we need her oil.
  (d) Send American troops only as part of a United Nations force.
  (e) Do not get involved. This is Kuwait's problem. American soldiers should
      not fight and die for this. America should not spend money on this.
  (f) Organize United Nations economic punishments for Iraq. Boycott Iraq.
      Stop buying Iraqi oil. Do not let Iraq receive supplies from anywhere.
  (g) Send money and supplies, but not troops.
  (h) Other: _____

● *Why did you decide that way? Plan how you will explain your decision to your classmates.*
  Write out your reasoning completely.

Name _____   Date _____

1990

American Citizens
Should English be the official language of the United States?

It is 1990. You are an American citizen. In the national and state legislatures, some representatives want to make English the official language of our country. They are trying to pass a constitutional amendment that makes <u>this</u> the law. Others are fighting this idea. They say it would be bad for the United States. Who is right?

PRO: It is important to have a common language that all Americans can understand. People need to know English. They have to be able to read, write, understand, and speak English so they can learn about the history, government, and culture of this country. There have always been immigrants in the U.S., but they always learned English. Now, in some places it seems as though you never hear English! We need this amendment to show new immigrants that the English language is important in America.

Another point is that bilingual services are expensive. Americans should not have to pay for translating documents into other languages or for teaching classes in other languages. It is cheaper if everyone living in this country uses English.

CON: Everybody knows English is important, so we do not need an official language. Immigrants want to learn English, but they should be able to keep and use their native languages, too. In school, American students study foreign languages for years! It would be a waste of time and money to ignore the

languages people already know. Besides, this law does not give more money to teach English as a Second Language. It will not help anyone learn English.

Some states and cities have already passed "official English" laws. In Florida, for example, the legislature recently amended the state constitution. Now English is the official language of Florida. The U.S. Constitution says that the state legislatures can make such laws, but what does this mean? Some people say that it means no more bilingual education for immigrants. Others say that hospitals, courts, and schools can offer services only in English and that employers can make rules forbidding employees from using languages other than English.

Would an official language amendment to the Constitution be good for our country?

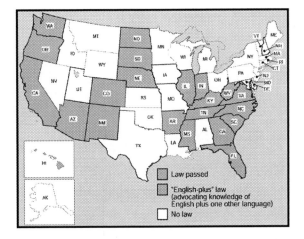

© 1997 J. Weston Walch, Publisher

American Citizens: Should English be the official language of the United States? *(continued)*

Comprehension

1. Who are you in this decision?

2. In paragraph 1, what does the word <u>this</u> refer to?

3. What would the new amendment say?

4. What are reasons in favor of making English the official language of the U.S.?

5. What are reasons against making English the official language of the U.S.?

6. Does the United States have an official language now?

7. What could change if this amendment passes?

Decision

- *Should English be the official language of the United States? Choose one or more of the following options:*

   (a) No. We have never had such a law, and we should not have it now.

   (b) Yes. English should be one official language, but there should be others as well.
       Which languages? _____

   (c) Yes, but only if the laws give more money to teach English as a Second Language.

   (d) No, not English. The official language(s) of the United States should be

       _____

   (e) Yes. English should be the only official language of the U.S.

   (f) Other: _____

- *Why did you decide that way? Plan how you will explain your decision to your classmates. Write out your reasoning completely.*

1992

U.S. Congress
Should the U.S. sign a free trade agreement with Canada and Mexico?

It is 1992. You are a member of Congress. President Bush has just finished negotiating the North American Free Trade Agreement (NAFTA) with our neighbors—Canada and Mexico. Now the president wants the Congress to approve this agreement. Before you vote, listen to what the president and other Americans say about NAFTA.

PRESIDENT BUSH: We need to guarantee foreign markets for American products. This free trade agreement will mean no import taxes on our products in Canada and Mexico. That will make our products cheaper in those places. Canadians and Mexicans will buy more American products. That means more jobs for American workers. This agreement will also make it easier for American companies to build factories in Mexico, where labor costs are low. Products made in Mexico cost less money, so American consumers can save money. The free trade agreement we signed with Canada two years ago has been good for America. NAFTA will bring the three North American countries closer together. In Asia and Europe, countries are signing free trade agreements like NAFTA. This agreement will protect American business and jobs from foreign competition.

BUSINESS LEADERS: President Bush is right. NAFTA will help us sell more products around the world. The Asian countries pay their workers less than workers are paid in America. That means that products made in

Asia cost less than American products. If our products are more expensive, nobody will buy them. With NAFTA, we can make things cheaply in Mexico and sell them around the world.

LABOR UNIONS: NAFTA is a big mistake. It is going to hurt American workers and Mexican workers, too. When American companies move to Mexico, they will close their factories here. They will hire Mexican workers, not Americans. The president says that consumers will benefit because prices will be lower. But workers are consumers, too. If we do not have jobs, we cannot buy any products! The business leaders say that NAFTA will be good for Mexican workers. That is a joke. The minimum wage in the U.S. is $4.65 an hour. In Mexico that is the wage for one day! The only reason the companies want to move to Mexico is to pay workers less money.

ENVIRONMENTALISTS: NAFTA might be good for business, but it will be bad for the environment. When the U.S. signed a free trade agreement with Canada a few years ago, some Canadian companies moved to the U.S. because the environmental laws here are not as strict as the laws in Canada. The same thing will happen now. Mexico does not have strong laws to protect the environment. The Canadian and American companies that move there will pollute the air and water. NAFTA does not say enough about protecting the environment.

Name _____ Date _____

Comprehension

1. Who are you in this decision?

2. How is NAFTA different from the agreement we already have with Canada?

3. Which U.S. groups are in favor of NAFTA?

4. What are three reasons why moving to Mexico could be good for American companies?

5. Why are U.S. workers against NAFTA?

6. Who makes more money—workers in the U.S. or workers in Mexico?

7. Which country has the strongest environmental laws—Mexico, Canada, or the U.S.?

8. What decision do you have to make?

Decision

- *How will you vote on NAFTA?*

   (a) Vote yes.

   (b) Vote no.

   (c) Suggest changes to make NAFTA better before you vote. What changes do you recommend? _____

   (d) Talk to people in Mexico and Canada before you vote. What questions will you ask them? _____

   _____

   (e) Other: _____

- *Why did you decide that way? Plan how you will explain your decision to your classmates. Write out your reasoning completely.*

U.S. Congress

Should Congress make it harder to buy handguns?

1993

It is 1993. You are a congressperson. Congress is ready to vote on the "Brady Bill." If Congress approves this bill, it will be more difficult for people to buy handguns. How will you vote? Americans have strong feelings about this bill. Here are some of the arguments you have heard:

CON: The Second Amendment to the U.S. Constitution says that Americans have the right to own guns.

PRO: Not true! The amendment says that the military has the right to have guns, not the people.

CON: There are lots of good reasons to have guns. Hunting and target shooting are sports. The government should not stop people from enjoying these sports.

PRO: Nobody uses handguns for hunting. For target practice, people can rent guns at shooting ranges. They are too dangerous to keep at home!

PRO: Guns are dangerous. There are too many accidents with handguns. Parents do not lock up their guns, and their kids accidentally shoot somebody. Also, guns are dangerous because they are so easy to use. Somebody gets angry and just picks up a gun and kills a person. Besides, if people did not have guns around, maybe there would not be so many suicides.

CON: *Guns* are not dangerous; *people* are. And people can be trained to use guns safely. More people are hurt or killed by falling down or drowning than by guns.

CON: People need guns for self-defense. If people have guns, they can protect themselves. Also, if criminals think that more people have guns, they will not attack. If we stop law-abiding people from having guns, only criminals will have guns.

PRO: Handguns are not good for self-defense. Most criminals say that guns don't stop them. Dogs stop them. Also, criminals often get their guns by breaking into houses and stealing them.

PRO: The U.S. has more handgun deaths than countries that have gun control laws. England and Japan, for example, have strict gun control laws, and they have very few shootings. In cities in America that have gun control laws, the crime rate has gone down.

CON: Not true! In England, the crime rate went up more than in the United States Massachusetts has a strict gun registration law, but Boston has the fifth highest crime rate in America! And New York City has a gun registration law, but there are 1 to 2 million *unregistered* guns in the city. The gun control laws do not work.

The people in your state who voted for you want you to do the right thing. How will you vote?

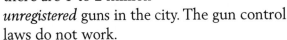

Name _____ Date _____

Comprehension

1. Who are you in this story?

2. For each statement, write *F* for fact or *O* for opinion. Remember that facts are things that can be checked and agreed to by everyone. Opinions are a person's own ideas.

   (a) The Second Amendment says that people have the right to own guns.

   (b) Hunting and target shooting are sports.

   (c) Handguns are too dangerous to keep at home.

   (d) There are many accidental shootings.

   (e) People can be trained to use guns safely.

   (f) People are careless with guns.

   (g) Criminals often steal guns from houses.

   (h) England and Japan have strict gun control laws.

   (i) The crime rate has gone down in cities that have gun control laws.

   (j) The gun registration law doesn't work in New York City.

3. What is the purpose of the Brady Bill?

Decision

● *How are you going to vote on this bill? Choose one of the following options:*

   (a) Vote for the Brady Bill. It should not be easy to get handguns.

   (b) Vote against the Brady Bill. It should be easy to get handguns.

   (c) Support another bill that makes all kinds of guns difficult to get.

   (d) Oppose all gun control bills. People have the right to own any kind of gun they want.

   (e) Oppose gun control bills. People who want to own guns will not vote for you in the future if you support this bill.

   (f) Other: _____

● *Why did you decide that way? Plan how you will explain your decision to your classmates. Write out your reasoning completely.*

Californians

Should California help people who come here illegally to live?

1994

It is 1994. You are a resident of California. State elections are coming up in a few days, and voters have a big decision to make: What rights should illegal immigrants have in California? Thousands of immigrants come here to live. Most come from Mexico and countries in Central and South America and Asia. Many do not have legal permission to be in the United States.

Now our state law says that anyone can attend public schools and use public hospitals in California. Governor Pete Wilson says that California and other border states are losing money. He says that the illegal immigrants do not pay taxes to help pay for schools and hospitals. The state government has to pay for these things. Wilson and other governors asked the federal government to give money to pay for the state services that illegal immigrants use. The government gave some money, but Wilson says it is not enough. He wants voters to approve a referendum called Proposition 187. If we approve it, only legal residents of the United States could use public services in California.

Some people think Proposition 187 will be bad for our state. There are several reasons. First, California's economy depends on immigrant labor. Most of the fruit and vegetables we sell to other states are picked by illegal immigrants. They do most of the work in restaurants and hotels, too. These jobs are hard and the pay is very low. Few Americans want to work in these jobs. Without immigrant labor, the prices we pay for these goods and services will rise quickly.

What will happen in the future if illegal immigrants cannot use public hospitals? If there is an epidemic, they will not have good health services. The disease could spread to everyone—even to citizens and legal residents. Also, school is a place where immigrant children learn about our country. If they cannot attend school, how will these children learn American history? How will they learn to communicate in English? If they do not receive a good education, they will not be able to get good jobs. Then they will never be able to pay taxes for services!

This law could be very difficult to enforce, too. How will schools and hospitals know who is here legally? This law could cause trouble for anyone who does not look or talk like an "American." Many doctors and teachers say they will not obey this law if it passes.

We are the most populous state in the U.S., and we have the most illegal immigrants, too. If California passes Proposition 187, other border states might make similar laws.

Name _____   Date _____

Californians: Should California help people who come here illegally to live? (continued)

Comprehension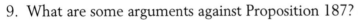

1. Who are you in this decision?
2. What other states have immigrant problems like ours?
3. Why do you think immigrants want to be in California?
4. Why do some immigrants come here illegally?
5. In paragraph 2, what does the word <u>it</u> refer to?
6. What kinds of work do illegal immigrants do in California?
7. What does Proposition 187 say?
8. What are some arguments in favor of Proposition 187?
9. What are some arguments against Proposition 187?
10. For each statement, write *T* for true or *F* for false:

    (a) The best way to tell if a person is American is to look at him or her and listen to that person speak.
    (b) The federal government gave California some money to solve this problem.
    (c) Other states could follow our example if Proposition 187 passes.

Decision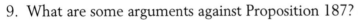

- *Should we vote "yes" on Proposition 187?*

    (a) Yes
    (b) We should let illegal immigrants use public hospitals but not schools.
    (c) We should let illegal immigrants use public schools but not hospitals.
    (d) No. We should not support Proposition 187.
    (e) We should ask the federal government to give us more money for the services illegal immigrants use.
    (f) Other: _____

- *Why did you decide that way? Plan how you will explain your decision to your classmates. Write out your reasoning completely.*

Historical Notes

1861—President Lincoln: How should we respond to the attack on Fort Sumter?

> ### Vocabulary
>
> | | |
> |---|---|
> | cannons | military |
> | civil war | surrender |
> | inauguration | to protect |
> | seceded | soldiers |

By March 1861, the Confederacy had taken all federal property within its boundaries except for Fort Pickens at Pensacola, Florida, and Fort Sumter. When Union Commander Robert Anderson refused Jefferson Davis's order to surrender the fort, Confederate guns placed around Charleston Harbor began shooting at a federal ship bringing supplies to the fort. With only a few days remaining as president, James Buchanan decided to do nothing (option *e*). After his inauguration on March 4, Lincoln also hoped to avoid a battle over the fort. Finally, on April 6, he announced he was sending another supply ship. The Confederate guns began firing on Fort Sumter on April 12. After 34 hours of shelling, the Union soldiers surrendered the fort (option *c*) and sailed to New York. Only one person was killed, but the attack on Fort Sumter is considered the beginning of the Civil War.

1865—Northern States: They killed Lincoln! How should we punish the South?

See also 1866—REPUBLICAN SENATOR.

> ### Vocabulary
>
> | | |
> |---|---|
> | assassinated | murderer |
> | assassins | make peace |
> | furious | punish |
> | unite | |

The Republican-dominated Congress was strongly critical of Lincoln's plan for readmission of the former Confederate states. The Republicans also assumed that Lincoln's assassination would increase public support for punishment of the defeated states. The new president, Andrew Johnson, used a congressional recess to begin implementing a plan very similar to Lincoln's (option *l*). By the end of 1865, all of the former Confederate states except Texas were ready to be readmitted to the Union. There was growing sentiment in Congress that Johnson had taken on powers belonging to Congress, as well as reports that southern whites were abusing the rights of freed blacks. With comfortable majorities in both houses after the elections of 1866, the Republicans enacted extensive civil rights legislation, including three constitutional amendments. The Thirteenth Amendment outlawed slavery in the U.S. (option *d*). The Fourteenth Amendment said that no state had the right to deprive people of their rights as citizens, that former rebels could not hold civil or military office (a form of option *i*), and that all states had to give up claims to war debts for damages (a form of option *b*). It also said that representation in the southern states would be based on the percentage of people who had remained loyal to the Union (a form of option *g*). The Fifteenth Amendment said that the voting rights of citizens could not be denied on the basis of color, race, or previous condition of servitude (option *h*).

In addition to the amendments, Congress also passed four Reconstruction Acts (1867–1868) over presidential veto. These acts divided the former Confederacy into five military districts. Federal soldiers occupied the southern states to ensure compliance with the conditions of their readmission (option *e*). Through agencies such as the Freedmen's Bureau, the government ran massive black voter registration drives (more option *h*). In 1867 there were 703,000 black voters and 627,000 white voters registered in the former Confederate states. Thaddeus Stevens, a Republican senator from Pennsylvania, proposed confiscating the lands of the richest rebels (option *j*) and redistributing it among the freedmen.

1866—Republican Senator: How can we make southern states obey the Constitution?

See also 1865—NORTHERN STATES.

Vocabulary

Republican senator	equal	Confederate
Congress	passing	Constitution
ratified	citizenship	guarantee
amendments	restrict	rights
slavery	abolished	obey
illegal		

Punishment of the rebellious southern states was part of Reconstruction, but so was genuine concern by many Republicans for the rights of blacks. Passage of the Thirteenth, Fourteenth, and Fifteenth Amendments indicated that Congress was dedicated to African American civil rights. The Republicans also stood to gain by adding over 700,000 potential voters to the roles. Unfortunately, Congress did not give freed slaves the economic support they needed to guarantee those rights. Many ex-slaves were more concerned with immediate economic needs in the devastated southern economy than they were with voting rights. Congress tied re-admission of rebel states to passage of the constitutional amendments. By 1870, all former states were back in the Union. Federal troops stayed in the South (option *f*) until 1877.

1868—Lakota: Should we sign the Fort Laramie Treaty?

Vocabulary

nation	obey	supplies
powerful	frightens	carpenter
Native Americans	plains	blacksmith
government	soldiers	engineer
a peace treaty	villages	promise
war chief	trust	reservation
steal	control	attack
hunting grounds	permission	property
truth	bother	

Red Cloud signed the Fort Laramie Treaty after a special council of chiefs granted him permission to speak for the Sioux. The Sioux's goal was to reopen trade with the whites along the Platte River. They had already achieved success in forcing the army to abandon the Bozeman Trail and its protective forts. The army's goal was to secure the Platte Valley route for trail and railroad development. The treaty was apparently deceptively communicated to the tribes, for trade was banned along the Platte, and the tribes were driven north of the river immediately after the signing. Tribes that tried to trade and tribes that lived south of the river were harassed and herded north into alien territory along the Missouri. The treaty declared that the tribes must live at agencies within the reservation, which was not what the natives had understood. Red Cloud and other chiefs went to Washington, D.C., and to New York, where their righteous and dignified plea for justice caused such an uproar that the government temporarily reversed its policy, giving permission to trade at Fort Laramie and a reservation near the fort on the Platte.

1870—Chinese Worker: Should you bring your family to America?

Vocabulary

accidents	decided	foreigners
boat tickets	finished	possible
dangerous	explosions	enough

Chinese immigration to the U.S. began with the California Gold Rush. In 1868, the need for rail-road laborers was so great that Congress passed the Burlingame Treaty, allowing unlimited Chinese immigration to the U.S. Despite earning lower wages than whites, Chinese workers flocked to the railroads being built across the western U.S. The number of Chinese immigrants living in the U.S. tripled in the period from 1867 to 1882, when the Chinese population peaked at 115,000.

1878—Southern Whites: How can we get our old way of life back? (Jim Crow laws)

Vocabulary

cooperating	politicians	rights
controlled	national	scalawags
Confederacy	government	state legislator
amended	presidential	soldiers
Constitution	election	Senate
carpetbag-	president	Republican party
gers	obey	public offices
abolished	ordered	swear
slavery	loyal	running for public
citizenship	House of Repre-	office
equal	sentatives	vote
force	occupied	
Democratic		

Many southern whites deeply resented the new amendments and presence of the federal troops enforcing them. The social and political order of the prewar South was turned upside down, with blacks holding many public offices. The participation in the state governments by northern "opportunists," while experienced and trusted southern leaders who had been in the Confederate government were barred from holding office, also rankled southern whites.

Federal troops occupied the states of the former Confederacy from 1867 to 1877, during which period the "Reconstruction" governments addressed a range of issues previously unthinkable in the South. For the first time, equality of education and voting rights were issues for all adult male citizens of the South. In the presidential election of 1876, Democratic candidate Samuel Tilden won the popular election but did not have enough votes in the electoral college. As a compromise to end the deadlock, Democrats agreed to let the Republican candidate, Rutherford B. Hayes, become the new President. In return, the Republicans promised to withdraw federal troops from the South.

With the soldiers gone, southern states lost little time in electing local and state officials and passing laws that contradicted the Fourteenth and Fifteenth Amendment (options *b* and *e*). Although slavery was no longer a legal institution, the freed slaves were forced, through a combination of repressive Jim Crow laws (options *b* and *e*) and physical intimidation by the Ku Klux Klan and other white supremacist groups, back into political and economic subjugation, which, despite progress during the civil rights movement in the 1960's, continues today.

1879—U.S. Congress: Should we restrict Chinese immigration?

See also 1870—CHINESE WORKER; 1948—U.S. FARM OWNERS; 1962—MIGRANT FARM WORKERS; 1994—CALIFORNIANS

Vocabulary

member	citizens	percent
Congress	population	limiting
immigrants	complaining	restrict
immigration	labor unions	businesses
federal government	grandchildren	treaty
trading partner		

Chinese immigration has long been a political issue for the U.S. The Burlingame Treaty of 1868 allowed unrestricted immigration from China but prohibited Chinese from becoming U.S. citizens (except by birth in the U.S). Congress passed the first of several "Chinese Exclusion Acts" in 1879, but the bill was vetoed by President Hayes. In 1880, the Chinese government agreed that the U.S. had the right to restrict (but not prohibit) immigration from China. In the early 1880's, white violence against Chinese people in western states increased, including the burning of the Chinatown section of Tacoma, Washington, and the killing of 28 Chinese in Rock Springs, Wyoming. In 1882, Congress passed and President Arthur signed into law a measure prohibiting immigration of Chinese laborers for 10 years (option *d*). With the passage of additional and more restrictive laws, many Chinese people left the U.S.

This decision, together with the decision "1870—Chinese Worker," can be compared to the series of decisions on labor needs and Mexican immigration. Students should appreciate the pattern that immigrant labor has been invited in economic boom times and pushed out during periods of recession.

1891—American Citizens: Should we protect our forests?

Vocabulary

citizen	conservationist	powerful
Congress	minerals	valuable
discussing	mining companies	to mine coal
passes	timber companies	steel
bill	percent	reserved
set aside	wildlife	industries
government	polluted	scenery
protect	natural resources	Act

The Forest Reserve Act passed in 1891. It empowered the president to set aside and reserve public forest lands. On opposite sides of the debate were the conservationist John Muir and Congressman Joseph Cannon, who once declared that the government should not spend one cent on scenery.

Some roles students could take in making this decision are congressperson, conservationist, lumberjack, Native American, miner/prospector, etc.

1892—Ida Wells: How can we stop the lynchings?

Vocabulary

citizens	protect	mobs
kidnap	town government	convince
torture	pay attention	trouble
lynching	consumers	shut down
hundreds	city streetcar system	white-owned
boycott	defend ourselves	federal

Lynching (to be hanged or otherwise killed without a trial) was a common fate for black males in the post-Reconstruction South. As part owner of *The Free Press*, Ida Wells regularly wrote editorials condemning white mobs lynching blacks. When three black businessmen were lynched in Memphis, Wells wrote a series of editorials calling on the town government to punish the killers and for blacks to boycott the Memphis streetcar system in protest. With the participation of black churches, the boycott was so successful that the streetcar company asked Wells to end it.

Angry whites burned Wells' newspaper press and warned her to leave Memphis and not return. Wells moved to New York City, where she worked for the *New York Age* newspaper and continued to speak and write in favor of civil rights for black Americans. She formed anti-lynching societies in England and the U.S.

1896—Supreme Court: Should the U.S. permit segregation? (Plessy v. Ferguson)

See also 1857—SUPREME COURT; 1954—SUPREME COURT.

Vocabulary

justice	colored	illegal
Supreme Court	arrested	separate but
segregation	section	equal
constitutional	guilty	marry
case	Amendments	continue
companies	Constitution	permit

Like Rosa Parks and the Montgomery bus strike 60 years later, Homer Plessy was a test case for civil rights groups. Although Plessy was seven-eighths white and only one-eighth black, the law considered him to be black. The Court's seven-to-one decision in favor of Ferguson and segregation (majority opinion by Justice Brown of Michigan and minority opinion by Justice Harlan of Kentucky) stressed the irrelevance of the Fourteenth Amendment to the case (option *b*), saying that segregation was legal because the Constitution did not tell people what to think.

The Court's decision legitimized the concept of "separate but equal," by which states could permit separate facilities for whites and blacks, so long as the facilities were equal. Facilities for blacks were almost never as good as facilities for whites, but the judicial precedent and social practice of "separate but equal" kept segregation in place throughout much of the South until the Plessy decision was overturned by the Court in Brown v Board of Education in 1954.

1896—President Cleveland: Should we make immigrants pass a literacy test?

See also 1974—SUPREME COURT.

Vocabulary

U.S. President	fail	education
term of office	veto	opportunity
decision	labor unions	supremacist
immigrants	wages	Protestants
literacy	strikebreakers	uneducated
Jewish	business owners	Catholic
Buddhist	physical labor	millions
political parties	elections	citizens
vote	muscles	

President Cleveland vetoed this bill in 1896, (option *d*), but similar legislation appeared before Congress seven times between 1896 and 1917. Bills were defeated three times in Congress and vetoed by Presidents Taft and Wilson. Finally, in 1917, Congress overrode Wilson's second veto. The Immigration Law required all immigrants over the age of 16 to be able to read at least 30 words in any language (option *b*), the only exception being for religious refugees. This law also excluded alcoholics and vagrants, raised the tax on incoming immigrants to eight dollars per person, and placed greater restrictions on the number of Asian immigrants.

1898—U.S. Congress: Should the U.S. go to war against Spain?

Vocabulary

member of Congress	revolution	leaders
battleship	soldiers	trade
exploded	citizens	million
sailors	powerful	plantations
responsible	empire	damaged
to declare war	independent	negotiate
foreign markets	blown up	defeat
Press	navy ship	rebels
support	export	territories
eventually	necessary	democracy
island	immediately	ports
military bases		

Although McKinley campaigned for the presidency as an anti-imperialist, he was eventually worn down by military and business leaders in favor of war. The popular press was strongly in favor of Cuban independence and, after the bombing of the U.S. battleship *Maine*, of the U.S. war against Spain. In April 1898, Congress voted in support of Cuban independence, demanded Spain's immediate withdrawal from Cuba, and gave President McKinley the authority to use the U.S. military to force Spain from the island. Under the Teller Amendment, Congress also specified that the U.S. would not annex Cuba. The measure passed 42 to 35 in the Senate and 311 to 6 in the House. Spain immediately declared war on the U.S.

As it turns out, one of the war's strongest supporters, Roosevelt, then Assistant Secretary of the Navy, had secretly put U.S. forces on alert in the Pacific to prevent the Spanish fleet in the Philippines from sailing to the defense of their forces in Cuba. Although the battle best remembered in history books is Roosevelt's cavalry charge up Kettle Hill in Cuba (which helped Americans win the Battle of San Juan Hill), American success in the war was mainly due to naval superiority. Within four months, Spain had surrendered. Despite the Teller Amendment, Congress passed subsequent legislation that forced Cuba to accept U.S. intervention at U.S. discretion. The U.S. then paid Spain $20 million as compensation for Puerto Rico, the Philippine Islands, and Guam. About 5,000 U.S. soldiers died during the Spanish-American War, mostly from disease.

1899—U.S. Congress: Should we control the Philippine Islands?

See also 1898—U.S. Congress.

Vocabulary

senator in the U.S. Congress	gold	freedom
	excellent	revolution
soldiers	crops	self-govern-ment
defeated	navy bases	
controls	militarily	thousands
ratify	economically	rebels
peace treaty	independent	army
million	welcomed	navy
territories	indepen-dence	crush
colony		missionaries
minerals	constitution	Christian
coal	foreign	

Unlike the decision to grant McKinley war powers to begin the war with Spain, there was serious debate in the Senate before the Treaty of Paris was narrowly approved. Although McKinley was strongly pressured by evangelical Christian groups to "save" the Philippines by annexation, his claim that Filipinos were unfit for self-rule should probably be seen as politically motivated. With the expulsion of the Spanish, Filipino leader Emilio Aguinaldo, brought out of exile by Dewey, began to establish constitutional government. This was too much self-government for the U.S., which then created military zones designed to keep the Filipinos outside the capital and out of power. Fighting between U.S. and Filipino forces broke out during the treaty hearings and may have convinced the Senate to vote for ratification.

It took two and a half years and $400 million to defeat the Filipinos. Seventy thousand American soldiers fought in the war and about 4,000 died. Eighteen thousand Filipino soldiers died in the fighting, and approximately 200,000 civilians died from famine and disease, the result of relocation and scorched earth policies by the Americans. At the end of the war in 1902, the Philippines became an unorganized U.S. territory. The country gained independence in 1946.

1905—Blacks: What is the best way for us to get social equality? (B. Washington or Du Bois)

Vocabulary

Constitution	solve	vote
carpenters	social equality	violence
amendments	Ku Klux Klan	tradespeople
demand civil rights	patient	to treat
college professor	racism	technical
guarantees	rights	college
discriminating	responsible	tradespeople
founder	ignore	

Washington and Du Bois represented two generations and two different perspectives on black–white relations in America. Washington, a former slave, was seen by whites as a spokesman for all blacks. His call for economic security before political and civil rights made sense to many blacks at a time when the federal government ignored blatant and widespread violation of the Fourteenth and Fifteenth Amendments. Du Bois was younger, northern-born, and had studied at Harvard and in Europe before moving to the South to teach. His appeal to blacks to push for political rights was supported by blacks who were tired of waiting for whites to give them equality.

In making this decision, students can take different roles: college student, sharecropper, northern and southern blacks, etc. This decision can be compared with the 1963 decision in which students consider the ideas of Martin Luther King and Malcolm X.

1908—Native Americans: Should we send our children to white people's schools?

See also 1810—CHEROKEE; 1974—SUPREME COURT; 1990—AMERICAN CITIZENS.

Vocabulary

hunt	difficult
religion	language

As whites encroached on their lands, Native Americans could fight, run away, or stay and make the best of it. By 1908, the first two options had been severely limited for most Native Americans. At this point in time, the Ojibway were being increasingly drawn into the cash economy. Public and mission schools offered cultural information and skills that were valued in the white world and were more financially rewarding than the traditional ways.

How children are educated says much about a society. Comparing this decision with others about education will reveal patterns and differences in American attitudes. Teachers may wish to write their own education decision based on a situation the students would recognize—"City Voters: Should we raise taxes to build a new high school?"

This decision is based on the book *Dream of the Great Blue Heron*.

1917—American Citizens: Should we get involved in the war in Europe? (World War I)

Vocabulary

armies	assassin	military
borders	leader	merchants
treaties	soldiers	citizen
allies	weapons	involved
attack	thousands	submarine
the Central	neutral	ammunition
Powers	governments	million
volunteer	supplies	

When war broke out in Europe in 1914, the U.S. proclaimed neutrality, while claiming the right to trade with both sides (option *g*) and demanding safe passage for transport and passenger ships. While the American government found the British naval blockage of Germany (including search and seizure of American ships) aggravating, it was the attacks on U.S. merchant ships by German U-Boats that eventually led to U.S. involvement in the war.

Wilson threatened war with Germany and demanded indemnification (option *c*) following the sinking of the *Lusitania*. Germany promised to stop U-Boat attacks on merchant vessels and to pay for the American lives and goods lost on the *Lusitania*.

Meanwhile, U.S. banks were lending $500 million to Britain and France in the form of credits for war materials (options *d* and *e*). With public sentiment against U.S. involvement in a foreign war, Wilson recognized that U.S. economic interests would be hurt by an Allied loss. He campaigned for re-election in 1916 on the slogan "He kept us out of war," while authorizing increased military spending (option *f*). When Germany resumed unrestricted submarine warfare in January 1917, Wilson broke off diplomatic relations. On March 18, three U.S. merchant ships were sunk by German U-Boats. To further build public support for U.S. entry into the war, Wilson released the "Zimmerman Note," an intercepted German plan which promised Mexico would receive territories lost to the U.S. in return for a Mexican declaration of war against the U.S. With public opinion behind him, Wilson asked Congress to declare war on Germany on April 2 (option *b*). It did so on April 6.

In the 18 months the U.S. was involved in the war, some 2.8 million American men were drafted, and over 115,000 died in Europe. The massive participation by U.S. troops and the financial support of the Allies were major factors in the Allied victory.

1919—U.S. Congress: Should America join the League of Nations?

See also 1945—AMERICAN CITIZENS.

Vocabulary

senator	join
U.S. Congress	foreign
terrible	approve
treaty	oppose
discuss	decide
alliances	

Wilson's dream of U.S. participation in a League of Nations was blocked by Republican Senate majority leader Henry Cabot Lodge. Although 33 governors had endorsed Wilson's plan, Lodge's position was popular with the American public so soon after a costly foreign war. During Wilson's long illness in 1919, Lodge attached changes to Article 10 of the plan (option *b*) during Congressional ratification of the Treaty of Versailles. The changes retained Congressional authority to decide the timing and circumstances of U.S. commitment to wars fought by other League members.

Wilson refused to compromise, and the Senate voted down his proposal in March 1920 (option *c*). The U.S. continued an isolationist foreign policy until the beginning of World War II. The U.S. joined the United Nations in 1945.

1920—Negroes in the South: Should we move north?

Vocabulary

segregated	owe
voting	debts
property	factories
rent	survive
contract	impossible
landlord	

In 1915, 75 percent of U.S. African Americans lived in the rural South. Of these, about 10 percent owned land; most of the rest worked as sharecroppers and seasonal laborers. In addition to dissatisfaction with poor education and difficult living conditions in the South, several changes contributed to the "Great Migration" of blacks to northern cities. In 1915, the boll weevil blight wiped out cotton crops across the lower South, making sharecropping even less economically feasible. The growth of new industrial centers such as Birmingham and Memphis, and service in World War I, brought money and new experiences to African Americans who had previously known only rural life.

As the first families to go north sent home letters with positive reports, the migration grew to such proportions that southern landowners became alarmed at the rapid loss of their traditional labor source. Some states passed legislation preventing blacks from traveling on northbound trains. Despite the financial and social costs of moving north, one million blacks did.

1920—State Legislators: Should women have the right to vote? (Nineteenth Amendment)

See also 1848—WOMEN AT SENECA FALLS.

Vocabulary

state legislators	the right to vote
elections	demanded
amend	Revolutionary
Constitution	Civil War
allow	abolition
ratify	prohibition movement
World War	run for public office
taking care of	democracy
citizens	

The women's suffrage movement began at the Seneca Falls Convention in 1846. Early suffragists gained political experience in the abolition and temperance movements, but women's suffrage was excluded when Congress adopted the Fifteenth Amendment. Following this defeat, suffragists worked on two fronts—to persuade state legislatures to adopt a suffrage amendment and to persuade the national Congress to do the same. The movement gathered strength in western states (women could vote in Colorado, Idaho, Utah, and Wyoming by 1896) and in cities where increasing numbers of educated and professional women compared their rights with those of men and women around the world. Tactics varied. Suffragists burned effigies of President Wilson, and they also gathered over 400,000 signatures on a pro-suffrage petition presented to Congress in 1914. Wilson seems to have come around to supporting women's suffrage as a result of women's support for the war movement. When Congress approved the amendment in 1919 and the required number of state legislatures also approved it by 1920, women could finally vote throughout the United States.

1935—President Roosevelt: What should the government do to help poor people during the Depression?

Vocabulary

President	businesses
elected	agriculture
depression	industry
failed	social problems
administration	improves
rent	savings
survive	government
business	

Believing that the measures to stimulate the economy taken early in his first term were working too slowly, Roosevelt announced the "Second New Deal" in 1935. With 10 million Americans unemployed, many of the new measures involved government spending to put people to work (option *c*), including the Works Progress Administration and the National Youth Administration. Projects like the Rural Electrification Act also guaranteed that there would be jobs building infrastructure. Roosevelt also established the Resettlement Administration, dedicated to buying land for the relocation of tenant farmers (option *g*). Another program helped people to buy back on favorable terms homes lost during the depression (option *f*). Encouraging Americans to work in other countries (option *h*) would probably

never have been an official policy, given the U.S.'s historic role as home for immigrants and temporary workers and the poor economic climate in most countries in the world at that time. Ironically, increased production and employment as a result of World War II did end the Depression.

1940—American Citizens: Should the U.S. get involved in World War II?

Vocabulary

conquered	arresting
Führer	imprisoning
soldiers	Jewish
defeated	allies
airplanes	involved
bombed	foreign
military	

Although American sympathy was clearly with the Allies, few Americans wanted to get into another world war. The U.S. casualties in the first one (more than 115,000 dead and more than 200,000 wounded) kept American foreign policy, formally at least, isolationist (option *a*). Early in 1940, Roosevelt took steps to increase British and French access to U.S. weapons (option *d*). This was the beginning of several creative projects by which the U.S. could support the Allies and still stay out of the war. The Lend-Lease Act of 1941 provided for massive quantities of weapons and military supplies to be "loaned" to Britain and the U.S.S.R. The U.S. military budget was increased to build more aircraft and warships, while old destroyers were traded off for rights to naval and air bases in the Atlantic (option *f*).

The U.S. entered the war upon the Japanese sneak attack on Pearl Harbor on December 7, 1941 (option *g*). On December 11, Germany and Italy declared war on the U.S. The fighting lasted until the atomic bombing of Hiroshima and Nagasaki. Three hundred thousand American soldiers died in the war. American participation probably saved Britain and the Soviet Union from defeat.

1942—American Citizens: Are Japanese Americans and other immigrants dangerous to our national security?

Vocabulary

soldiers	mayor
immigrants	the West Coast
loyal	religion
former	attack
enemies	crazy
trust	volunteered
government	

Immigrants and minorities of all backgrounds served in the U.S. military in World War II. There was no widespread perception of German Americans (unlike in World War I) and Italian Americans as possible traitors. Japanese Americans were perceived differently for several reasons: Japanese immigration was heavily concentrated on the West Coast; the government had already stopped Japanese immigration with the Immigration Exclusion Act (1924); there was an American racism against nonwhites and non-Europeans; and the Japanese had bombed Pearl Harbor in December 1941.

Immediately after the Japanese attack, FBI agents arrested 2,000 Japanese aliens (option *g*). After swearing a loyalty oath to the U.S. (option *c*), most were released. Strange signals attributed by the army to Japanese Americans trying to guide Japanese planes to the California coast were disproved by FBI investigations. In February 1942, Roosevelt signed Executive Order 9066, providing for removal and internment of 110,000 Japanese Americans from the West Coast to camps in Arkansas, Arizona, Colorado, Iowa, and Wyoming (option *d*). (Japanese Americans in Hawaii were not interned, although the population there was much larger.) Most families had little time to sell or store their possessions before being taken to the camps. In the camps, Japanese Americans were required to swear loyalty to the U.S. (option *c*).

In 1944, the Supreme Court ruled that the internment was constitutional. In 1945, the Court added that the government could not hold Japanese Americans who had sworn loyalty to the United States. Thousands of Japanese American men served in the U.S. military during the war, and no Japanese Americans were convicted of acts of sabotage during the war. In the 1980's, some of those interned sought to redress the wrongs they had suffered during the war. The Commission on Wartime Relocation and Internment of Civilians recommended that each internment survivor be given $20,000 compensation. Some Japanese Americans successfully sought to have their criminal records erased.

1945—American Citizens: Should the U.S. join the United Nations?

Vocabulary

citizen	decisions	solutions
surrendered	organization	Security
continues	purpose	Council
soldiers	avoid	solve
civilians	disagreements	keep peace
wounded	standard of living	Court of Justice
trillions	charter	settle
delegates	General Assembly	Economic and
nations	economic devel-	Social Council
international	opment	human rights
sponsor	Senate	compromises
troops	recommend	

See also 1919—U.S. CONGRESS.

Conferences at Dumbarton Oaks (Washington, D.C.) and Yalta established plans for the U.N. charter and initial agreements. One concession made at Yalta provided that Russia, the Ukraine, and Byelo-Russia would all have votes in the General Assembly, thereby giving the U.S.S.R. three votes, as mentioned in the vignette. The Russians had initially wanted 16 votes, one for each republic, to offset the Western bloc. The real power lay in membership and voting in the Security Council, however, since permanent members have veto power. The Senate passed the United Nations Participation Act. It even specified that the president was not required to seek congressional approval for U.N.-sponsored economic sanctions or to provide military forces requested by the Security Council.

1945—President Truman: Should the U.S. drop the atomic bomb on Japan to end the war?

Vocabulary

Japanese soldiers	promised	weapon
atomic bomb	terrible	several
continuing	prevent	Soviet Union
surrender	injured	scientists
powerful	condition	rule
military target		

On August 5, 1945, the U.S. B-29 bomber *Enola Gay* dropped a uranium bomb on the city of Hiroshima, a military-industrial center. At least 70,000 people were killed directly and indirectly as a result of the explosion, firestorm, and radioactive fallout from the bomb. When no answer was received from Japan, Truman ordered a second bomb dropped on Nagasaki, an important port city, on August 9. Japan accepted U.S. and Allied terms of "unconditional surrender." The U.S. did not insist on its earlier demand that Emperor Hirohito be deposed. U.S. military occupation of Japan began almost immediately under General Douglas MacArthur and ended in 1952 when Japan regained its sovereignty.

When he assumed the presidency following Roosevelt's death, Truman knew about the Allied decision (negotiated at Potsdam) to press for unconditional Japanese surrender, but he was unaware of the Manhattan Project and the existence of the atomic bomb. Prior to Hiroshima and Nagasaki, the U.S. had been carrying out firebombing of Japanese cities. Millions of Japanese civilians died in these night raids. It seems clear, given U.S. military superiority, promise of Soviet reinforcements, and ongoing U.S. firebombing of Japanese cities, that Japan's surrender was imminent. The "official" troop count of American lives to be saved has also been questioned. The world was horrified by the bombings. Some historians credit this horror with ensuring that atomic bombs have not been used since 1945.

1947—Truman Administration: Should America help rebuild Europe? (Marshall Plan)

See also 1917—AMERICAN CITIZENS; 1940—AMERICAN CITIZENS.

Vocabulary

member	civilians	soldiers
president	hundred	recover
cabinet	thousand	trading partner
billions	situation	repair
disaster	products	afford
atomic bombs	unstable	Secretary of State
allies	economic	Soviets
factories	situation	territories
destroyed	socialism	Hiroshima
bridges	communism	Nagasaki
damaged	Soviet Union	Secretary of
rebuilding	enemies	Agriculture
general	millions	wiped out
Czechoslovakia		

After six months of debate, the Truman administration convinced Congress that rebuilding Europe was the best way to guarantee America's position as the world's richest and most powerful nation. Originally, money was offered to all European nations affected by the war, including the Soviet bloc (option *c*). The Soviets, whose earlier requests for loans had been ignored by the U.S., pressured the countries under their control not to participate in what became known as the Marshall Plan. During the period 1948 to 1952, the U.S. gave $17 billion to 16 cooperating European nations, including Italy and West Germany. The plan included supplies of food and other essential consumer items, reconstruction of the agricultural and industrial base of Europe, as well as the lowering of certain U.S. tariffs (option *f*). The Marshall Plan accelerated the restoration of European economies to their prewar capacities. After 1952, foreign aid was increasingly used to build military support in noncommunist nations.

Students can take different roles as they discuss the merits of Marshall's plan: businessperson, farmer, banker, military general, etc. This decision and the logic behind it can be compared to others involving foreign aid.

1948—U.S. Farm Owners: How can we get cheap labor to work on our farms? (Migratory Labor Agreement)

See also 1685—COLONIAL PLANTER; 1796—SOUTHERN PLANTER; 1870—CHINESE WORKER; 1962—MIGRANT FARM WORKERS; 1980—AMERICAN CITIZENS; 1994—CALIFORNIANS.

Vocabulary

population	crops	legally
agriculture	insurance	illegal
machines	benefits	profits
pick fruit	temporary	immigration
vegetables	federal govern-	tractors
harvest	ment	wages

There is a long tradition of Mexican migrant labor in the U.S. During World War I, the Labor Department relaxed the restriction limiting Mexican migrants to agricultural work. During World War II, Mexican workers picked U.S. crops to fill the labor gap left by men who had gone to war. The Migratory Labor Act of 1942 brought contract workers known as "braceros" (helping hands) to work in the U.S. on temporary labor visas. When their work was finished, the Mexicans were supposed to return to Mexico. Jobs were scarce in Mexico, so many stayed. Between 1948 and 1964, approximately 5 million

Mexicans had entered the U.S. for temporary work. The peak year was 1956, when half a million contract workers worked on farms in 28 states. In seeking temporary, seasonal laborers, the farm owners and U.S. government had not counted on the large number of illegal immigrants who came to the U.S. Operation Wetback (1953–54) deported over 1 million illegal aliens, the great majority of whom were migrant laborers from Mexico.

The northward flow of labor from Mexico is based on supply and demand. Surplus Mexican laborers continue to do work that Americans cannot or will not do. In good economic times and in times of national emergency, the United States has consistently welcomed Mexican labor. In bad economic times, Americans have resented the presence of Mexican workers. The most recent example of this pattern is the passage of Proposition 187 in California. A similar issue is raised by Southeast Asian refugees.

This decision and others on immigration can help students appreciate how the economic climate can change social policy. Good resources to use with this decision are the movie *La Bamba* and Woody Guthrie's song "Deportee." Students might also think about what jobs in their community are held by a particular ethnic group and speculate why.

1950—President Truman: Should the U.S. fight communism in Korea?

See also 1964—Congressperson; 1950—State Department Worker; 1961—Kennedy; 1962—Kennedy; 1974—U.S. Congress.

Vocabulary		
president	bombs	ships
invaded	atomic	ground
divided	civilians	troops
reunite	military leaders	United
soldiers	communist govern-	Nations
	ment	weapons

Truman decided to wait until the U.N. Security Council voted on the South Korean request for aid (option *f*). (The U.S. and U.S.S.R. frequently vetoed each other's proposals before the Security Council voted, but on this occasion the Soviets boycotted the vote to protest U.N. recognition of Nationalist China.) The Security Council voted to send a U.N. force to aid South Korea, but while the 16 member countries prepared their troops, Truman authorized General Douglas MacArthur to land U.S. troops in

Korea (option *g*). These "U.N. forces" rapidly pushed the North Korean army out of South Korea and almost to North Korea's border with China. China sent 200,000 soldiers into Korea, forcing the U.S./U.N. forces back to the border between North and South Korea. When MacArthur publicly criticized the president for not bombing Chinese troops, Truman recalled him as head of U.N. forces.

The fighting lasted three years before ending in a stalemate between North and South in 1953. Fifty-four thousand U.S. soldiers and about 2 million Koreans, including many civilians, died in the war. The border between North and South Korea remains where it was in 1953. It is one of the most heavily armed borders in the world today.

Doing this decision in tandem with the other 1950 decision (State Department Worker) allows students to consider Senator Joseph McCarthy's assertion that communism was a greater threat from inside the U.S. than from the outside.

1950—State Department Worker: What should you tell the Senate Foreign Relations Committee? (McCarthy hearings)

See also 1950—President Truman.

Vocabulary		
communism	government	Republican
Communist Party	employee	senator
atomic bomb	Fifth Amendment	revolution
enemy	freedom of speech	enough
attention	State Department	punish
appear	political beliefs	refuse
message	Foreign Relations Committee	reputation
		spread

Students need to know what communism is before doing this decision. The Chinese Revolution was beyond the ability of the U.S. to control. However, it caused many Americans to believe McCarthy's charges that the State Department was sympathetic to communism. For four years, Joseph McCarthy kept the issue of communist infiltration of the government and military in the U.S. press. His accusations began in a speech in Wheeling, West Virginia, in February 1950, in which McCarthy claimed to have the names of 205 communists in the State Department. Pressed by the Senate to give names, McCarthy changed the number several times before it was disclosed that most of the people on his "list" had already left government employment.

Nevertheless, the Senate permitted McCarthy to question State Department and other government employees. In its report, the Tydings Committee said that McCarthy had imposed "a fraud and a hoax" on the Senate. In 1952, McCarthy became Chairman of the Senate Committee on Government Operations. He used the Investigations Subcommittee as a forum for denouncing communism in government. When McCarthy charged army officials with treason and communist sympathies, the televised hearings convinced many Americans that McCarthy had gone too far. He was censured by the Senate in 1954.

1954—Supreme Court: Should America have segregated schools?

See also 1896—SUPREME COURT; 1905—BLACKS; 1955—NEGROES IN MONTGOMERY, ALABAMA.

Vocabulary

justice	guarantee	"separate but
facilities	conditions	equal"
hospitals	disagree	Supreme Court
fountains	federal govern-	separate
constitutional	ment	railroad cars
equal	right	segregated

Following a string of civil rights victories in federal courts, the N.A.A.C.P. picked the Brown case (Brown v. Board of Education) as the one that would finally end segregation in public education. In contending that the Topeka, Kansas, school board had forced plaintiff Linda Brown to attend an inferior school because she was African American, Thurgood Marshall asked the Court to strike down the practice of "separate but equal."

Psychologist Kenneth Clarke demonstrated to the justices that black children were being hurt by attending segregated schools. The Court ruled unanimously that separate educational facilities were inherently unequal and that segregated schools violated the equal protection clause of the Fourteenth Amendment (option *a*). This overturned the Court's 1896 decision, Plessy v. Ferguson, that states could maintain separate facilities as long as they were equal (option *b*).

The Court did not specify how thousands of U.S. schools would be desegregated. The Brown decision angered many in the South, who felt that the national government was infringing on the rights of states to determine their own policies (option *c*).

Eventually, police and National Guard soldiers had to be brought in when white parents, politicians, and school officials refused to allow blacks to attend formerly white public schools. Later desegregation battles have centered on court-ordered busing as a means of integrating northern schools.

Students can compare this and other decisions of the civil rights movement of the 1950's and 60's with the federal decision to protect the constitutional rights of African Americans during Reconstruction. The documentary film *The Shadow of Hate* (1995, Teaching Tolerance) shows footage of desegregation following the Brown decision.

1955—Negroes in Montgomery, Alabama: Should we join the bus boycott?

See also 1905—BLACKS; 1954—SUPREME COURT; 1963—NEGRO COLLEGE STUDENTS.

Vocabulary

difficult	leaders	tried
dangerous	illegal	segregated
allow	protest	unconstitutional
arrested	public transportation	violence
court	protect	taxis
boycott		worth it

The Women's Political Council, supported by the N.A.A.C.P., organized the bus boycott. Prominent Negroes formed the Montgomery Improvement Association, which chose Dr. Martin Luther King, a minister and a newcomer to Montgomery, to lead the action. The bus boycott lasted 381 days, during which time the city tried to outlaw the boycott, whites bombed four black churches and several ministers' homes, and the bus company lost 65 percent of its business. Negroes formed car pools, black taxi companies carried Negroes for the price of a bus seat, and many simply walked. Finally, on November 13, 1956, the Supreme Court ruled that the state segregated-seating law was unconstitutional. The boycott demonstrated that peaceful, nonviolent resistance could succeed and that poor and middle class blacks could effectively and successfully protest segregation.

1961—U.S. Congress: Should we spend more money on space exploration?

Vocabulary

budget	program	services
exploration	national government	technology
outer space	military	rocket
disagree	planets	valuable
develop	Congress	minerals
solve		

The National Aeronautics and Space Administration (NASA) was created by the Eisenhower administration in 1958 in response to the Soviet satellite *Sputnik*. Kennedy's proposal to put "a man on the moon" was new, because it committed the U.S. to vastly increasing NASA's budget (option *b*).

Kennedy's goal of "beating the Russians to the moon" was realized in 1969. The military and scientific benefits of space exploration to date outweigh the benefits to consumers through product development. There has been no commercial exploitation of minerals from the moon. The cost of space exploration has recently led NASA to collaborate with space programs of other countries, including the former Soviet Union. The option of cost sharing is not included in this decision so that students may suggest it.

Gil Scott Herrin's poem "Whitey on the Moon" questioned whether money should be spent on space exploration when many Americans were suffering economic problems.

1961—President Kennedy: Should the U.S. invade Cuba? (Bay of Pigs)

See also 1962—PRESIDENT KENNEDY.

Vocabulary

foreign policy	companies	trade agreement
decision	invade	trained
government	communist	revolution
island	neighbor	soldiers
exiles	predecessor	support
attack	president	vacations
illegal	promised	successful
object	interfere	socialist
properties	secret plan	

Although begun under Eisenhower, the U.S.-sponsored invasion of Cuba at the Bay of Pigs on April 17, 1961, was a military and public defeat for Kennedy's presidency. The 1,500 Cuban exiles were easily defeated by Cuban forces, and no anti-Castro revolt materialized. Some 1,100 invaders were ransomed by the U.S. for $50 million in 1962. U.S.-Cuban relations continued to deteriorate, pushing Castro's government into closer alliance with the Soviet Union.

1962—President Kennedy: What should the U.S. do about the Soviet missiles in Cuba?

See also 1945—PRESIDENT TRUMAN; 1961—PRESIDENT KENNEDY.

Vocabulary

president	attack	to make a deal
trouble	suddenly	remove
spy planes	advisers	border
nuclear missile	surround	promise
bases	blockade	millions
delivered		

The Cuban missile crisis was the closest that the U.S. and U.S.S.R. ever came to a nuclear war. Kennedy was determined to appear strong in light of the failed Bay of Pigs invasion of Cuba in 1961. Kennedy cabled Khrushchev to warn him that the Soviet ships would be repelled (a combination of options *b* and *d*). For a few very tense days, it seemed that neither side would give in. The first relief came when Khrushchev announced that the Soviet ships would turn back in return for a U.S. pledge not to invade Cuba (option *g*). In the end, the deal also included the dismantling of the Soviet missile base in Cuba and a U.S. promise to remove its nuclear missiles in Turkey near the Soviet border (option *h*). The longer range of newer missiles meant that the U.S. missiles in Turkey and the Soviet missiles that nearly reached Cuba were no longer strategically necessary.

1962—Migrant farm workers: How can we get better working conditions?

See also 1948—FARM OWNERS.

Vocabulary

migrant	government	wages
legal right	organize	refuse
illegally	union	products
working conditions	join together	organize
improve	conditions	trouble
complain	demand	powerful

Except for brief periods during World War I and World War II, Mexican workers entering the U.S. were channeled into agricultural jobs. Many illegal workers were tolerated, even welcomed, as farm workers, but not in other jobs (option *f*). The seasonal, temporary nature of agricultural work made working in the U.S. (option *a*) and returning to Mexico (option *g*) a continuing cycle for many migrants.

Gains by migrant workers have come as a result of various strategies. In 1913, a protest in Wheatland, California, against poor living conditions led to a riot. In the 1920's, migrant workers in California organized the Confederacion de Uniones Obreras Mexicanos with 3000 members and 20 local chapters (option *c*). The most famous and successful union, the United Farm Workers Union, was founded by migrant worker and organizer Cesar Chavez in 1962. The U.F.W. used strikes (option *d*), marches, and hunger strikes to demand better conditions for grape pickers. In 1968, they began a nationwide boycott (option *e*) of non-union-grown grapes, later extended to lettuce and other farm products. In 1975 California passed a law requiring farm owners to bargain collectively with elected union officials. Higher wages and better living and working conditions were the results of the labor struggles by migrant workers. The increased costs of fruits and vegetables are passed on to consumers.

1963—Police Officer: What rights do people have if they are accused of a crime? (Miranda)

See also 1787—CONSTITUTIONAL CONVENTION; 1789—JAMES MADISON.

Vocabulary

arrested	right	committed
charged	lawyer	crime
kidnapping	guilty	criminal
raping	court	prison
lying	admit	questioning
Bill of Rights	police officer	accused

Miranda was found guilty based on his written confession after two hours of questioning. On appeal two years later, the Supreme Court decided that the Fifth Amendment against involuntary self-incrimination was incorporated into the Fourteenth Amendment, thereby applying to both state and federal courts. The Court decided that his confession was involuntary if he had not been fully and clearly informed of his Fifth Amendment rights or if he had not waived those rights voluntarily. The Court overturned Miranda's conviction by a vote of five to four.

(In contrast, English and European courts allow such evidence to be used, but the police officers are punished for gathering it illegally.)

Miranda was tried again and convicted on the basis of an admission he had made to his girlfriend. He returned to prison and was released nine years later. Four years later, he was stabbed to death in a barroom fight.

The "Miranda Rules" state that the local police must inform an accused person of his or her rights, which are:

1. You have a right to remain silent and do not have to say anything at all.
2. Anything you say can and will be used against you in court.
3. You have a right to talk to a lawyer of your own choice before we ask you any questions, and also to have a lawyer here with you while we ask questions.
4. If you cannot afford to hire a lawyer, and you want one, we will see that you have one provided to you free of charge before we ask you any questions.
5. If you are willing to give us a statement, you have a right to stop any time you wish.

1963—Negro College Students: Whom should we follow—Martin Luther King or Malcolm X?

See also 1955—Negroes in Montgomery, Alabama; 1905—Blacks; 1954—Supreme Court.

Vocabulary

slavery	nonviolence	violent
illegal	attacked	tolerance
government	register to vote	conquer racism
civil rights	fire hoses	discrimination
demand	control	defend
organized	police departments	educate
minister	pollute	black-owned
peaceful		

For many Americans, black and white, the ideals of gaining civil rights through nonviolence and peaceful integration were symbolized by Dr. Martin Luther King, Jr. In contrast, Malcolm X represented the views that blacks should not "turn the other cheek" to white violence, and that integration with whites was unhealthy for African Americans. King's following came from the rural South and from the black middle class, while Malcolm's primary appeal came from the urban North. As can be imagined, King's message of social harmony and integration was more easily accepted by whites than Malcolm's ideas.

Both men were assassinated in their late 30's, Malcolm in 1965 and King in 1968. At the time of their deaths, both leaders were going through a change in their thinking. King, for whom the goal of civil rights had depended on convincing mainstream America that the cause was correct, began to speak out against the Vietnam War and poverty in America, stances which alienated him from white supporters. On a pilgrimage to Mecca, Malcolm saw whites and blacks worshiping together and became convinced that integration of the races was possible.

1964—President Johnson: What is the government's role in fighting poverty?

See also 1935—President Roosevelt.

Vocabulary

president	nutrition	senior citizens
factories	military and foreign	federal taxes
producing	aid	inexpensive
products	preschool programs	reduces
percent	health care	medical care
poverty	programs	volunteer
difficulty	federal government	telephones
create	guaranteed mini-	televisions
facilities	mum wage	transportation

Lyndon Johnson capitalized on his experience in Congress to go far beyond the social programs begun by Kennedy. The Great Society, as Johnson called it, was the most ambitious body of social legislation since the New Deal. Johnson's self-proclaimed "war on poverty," run by the Office for Economic Opportunity, included the following programs: personal income tax cut (option *b*); Medicaid and Medicare health care programs for low-income and elderly Americans (option *d*); government scholarships and guaranteed loans to college students (option *f*); the Head Start Program (option *g*); construction of affordable housing in inner cities (option *h*); construction of national infrastructure to stimulate employment (option *k*); raise in the national minimum wage from $1.25 to $1.40/hour (option *n*); passage of the Urban Transportation Act to build mass transit in cities (option *l*); Job Core and VISTA programs (option *m*).

Despite the wide variety of antipoverty programs, Johnson's "war on poverty" was criticized for failing to challenge the fundamental systems in American society that made poverty so widespread in the first place. Another criticism was that Johnson's plan did not budget enough money to help 30 or 40 million Americans out of poverty. Some Great Society programs, notably Head Start and Medicare/Medicaid, remain in place today.

1964—U.S. Congress: Should the U.S. fight communism in Vietnam?

See also 1968—Vietnam Protesters; 1965—Conscientious Objectors; 1969—President Nixon; 1980—American Citizens; 1987—U.S. Congress.

Vocabulary

senator	North Vietnamese	communist
Congress	attacked	anticommunist
defend	Southeast Asia	enemies
soldiers	House of Represen-	believes
allies	tatives and the	dominoes
freedom	Senate	divided
millions	independence	weapons
debating	military advisers	involved
separate	civil war	jungles

The Gulf of Tonkin incident resulted in the Tonkin Gulf Resolution (choice *a*), which the House passed without dissent and the Senate passed 88 to 2. This began the U.S.'s escalation of and full-scale involvement in the war. The Senate Foreign Relations Committee investigated the Tonkin Gulf incident in 1968 and questioned the accuracy of Johnson's report. The Pentagon Papers further pointed out Johnson's manipulation of the incident to gain war powers. The Tonkin Gulf Resolution was repealed in January 1971. War was never declared by the U.S. The U.S. pulled out in 1973, and the war ended in 1975.

Over 50,000 Americans and 3,000,000 Vietnamese died in the war.

1965—Conscientious Objector?: What can you do if you oppose this war but your government wants you to fight?

See also 1964—U.S. CONGRESS; 1968—VIETNAM PROTESTERS.

Vocabulary

draft board	conscientious objectors	homosexual
join	civil war	handicapped
military	soldiers	pacifist
religion	destroyed	wounded
reason	Bible	supplies
defend	prison	continue
attacking		

The Selective Service Act of 1917 defined conscientious objectors as being people who belonged to "well-recognized" religious organizations with pacifist creeds. CO's did alternative service.

During World War II, legislation recognized conscientious objectors from other sects, as well. In 1970, the Supreme Court granted CO status to a nonreligious pacifist but in 1971 refused to grant CO

status to people objecting to specific wars, as in this case. Nevertheless, many young men had to make these choices.

1968—Vietnam War Protesters: How can we stop the war in Vietnam?

See also 1964—U.S. CONGRESS; 1965—CONSCIENTIOUS OBJECTOR; 1969—PRESIDENT NIXON; 1980—AMERICAN CITIZENS.

Vocabulary

citizen	Vietnamese	representatives
oppose	soldiers	jail
distrust	national leaders	support
leaders	attacking	troops
destroyed	defend	weapons
civilians	civil war	nuclear bombs
battles	control	protesters
captured	peace	communism
millions	taxes	

Choices *a* and *b*, along with many other forms of protest, such as working for draft information centers, were made. Many people were also confused by the government's stance and were unwilling to take actions that would seem unsupportive of the soldiers in combat.

1969—President Nixon: Should we bomb the communist Vietnamese camps in Cambodia?

See also 1964—U.S. CONGRESS; 1968—VIETNAM PROTESTERS; 1965—CONSCIENTIOUS OBJECTOR; 1980—AMERICAN CITIZENS.

Vocabulary

president	negotiating	jungle
honor	pulling out	commander
troops	involvement	permission
protesting	peace movement	neutral
enemy	commanders	foreigners
activities	central military	communist
villages	offices	headquarters
border		

The U.S. secretly began bombing on March 18, 1969 (choice *a*). The first bombing was not discovered by the press or protested by Prince Sihanouk. Over the next 14 months, 3,630 B-52 bombing raids were conducted along the Vietnam-Cambodia border. In April 1970, more than 70,000 American and South Vietnamese troops pushed into Cambodia. On April 30, 1970, President Nixon announced that U.S. and Vietnamese troops had entered Cambodia. Protests broke out across the U.S. The communist headquarters were never found.

1970—State Legislators: Should we lower the voting age to 18?

See also 1866—REPUBLICAN SENATOR; 1878—SOUTHERN WHITES; 1905—BLACKS; 1920—NEGROES IN THE SOUTH; 1920—STATE LEGISLATORS.

Vocabulary

member	property	responsible
ratify	national	state legislature
soldiers	government	thousands
drafting	Constitution	voting age
military	decided	amendment
issues	federal election	citizens

Teachers may want to help students understand that the *legal* right to vote has not always meant that everyone qualified has been allowed to cast a ballot. The timeline for this decision shows that the federal government extended suffrage to all male citizens over age 21 in 1866. However, as shown in the 1866 and 1897 decisions in this book, many state and local governments in the U.S. made it impossible for African Americans to practice their constitutional right to vote.

In 1971, Congress ratified the Twenty-sixth Amendment, lowering the voting age to 18 (option *b*). This added millions of potential new voters to the rolls. Although some politicians pitch campaigns to the "youth vote," the 18- to 21-year-old voting block routinely votes less often than do older Americans. Although people gain their legal majority at age 18, the Twenty-sixth Amendment provides only for voting rights. States retain the power to establish minimum age requirements in other areas, including the right to drive, the minimum age for leaving school and marrying, and the right to purchase alcohol and cigarettes.

1971—Supreme Court Justice: Should capital punishment be legal in the United States?

See also 1789—JAMES MADISON.

Vocabulary

justice	robbery	to sentence
arguments	kidnapping	criminals
Supreme Court	treason	commit
capital punish-ment	arson	insane
allow	permit	uneducated
death penalty	put to death	innocent
Amendment	death row	prisons
prohibits	lawyers	unconstitutional
cruel and unusual	violent	illegal
	helpless	Constitution

The Supreme Court decided five to four that capital punishment was unconstitutional because the death sentence had been arbitrarily applied, and this was "cruel and unusual punishment" (choices *b* and a form of *c*). Execution itself was not found to be cruel and unusual punishment. Mandatory and automatic sentences would probably still be constitutional. The Court's decision motivated state legislatures to rewrite capital punishment statutes. In 1976, the court allowed states to resume capital punishment, and 38 states have reinstituted it. In the 20 years that followed, 290 people were executed, three quarters of them in Texas, Florida, Virginia, Louisiana, Georgia, Alabama, and Arkansas. Nearly 3,000 inmates are on death row today.

1973—Supreme Court Justice: Should abortion be legal? (Roe v. Wade)

Vocabulary

justice	challenging	infections
issue	lawyers	rights to privacy
abortion	cases	protect
pregnant women	private	unborn fetus
remove	decisions	conception
allow	Constitution	travel
pregnancy	illegal	Supreme Court
legal	afford	

The two decisions, Roe v. Wade (Texas) and Doe v. Bolton (Georgia), were struck down in the 1973 decision with a seven to two Supreme Court vote. The Texas law was found to be too restrictive because it did not permit abortion in cases of rape or

incest. The Georgia law was found to be too
complex because it required a hospital board to
certify the abortion. The court decided that states
could not limit abortions during the first trimester of
pregnancy, the decision being "left to the medical
judgment of the doctor." Second trimester abortions
could be regulated to protect the woman's health;
states could legislate to regulate or prohibit third
trimester abortions, the stage of "viability," to protect
the fetus.

Abortion continues to be one of the most
controversial issues in America, with public support
for Supreme Court justices and political candidates
often based on the candidates' stance on abortion.
Among the issues in the ongoing debate: public
funding for abortions for poor women, abortions for
minors without parental consent, and federal protection of doctors and clinics performing abortions.

1974—U.S. Congress: Is the president of the United States above the law? (Watergate)

See also 1974—PRESIDENT FORD.

Vocabulary

congressperson	conversations	Senate
House of Repre-	refused	appointed
sentatives	special privileges	committee
serious	Supreme Court	investigation
impeach	mistake	erased
president	FBI	Republican
broke into	burglars	admitted
stealing	immediately	judge
Democratic	reelected	illegal
National	guilty	trial
Committee	court	

The correct sequence of comprehension question 19 is as follows: 3,1,5,8,10,2,7,6,9,11,12,4.

The House Judiciary Committee approved a
bill of impeachment citing obstruction of justice,
abuse of power, and refusal to comply with the
committee's subpoenas. President Nixon admitted
on August 5, 1974, that he had not fully and
correctly informed his attorneys or the Judiciary
Committee of all the facts, which amounted to
obstruction of justice. Realizing that impeachment
was certain, Nixon resigned the presidency on
August 9, 1974, and Gerald Ford was sworn in. One
month later, Ford fully pardoned Nixon for all
Watergate-associated offenses.

1974—President Ford: Should you pardon Richard Nixon?

See also 1974—U.S. CONGRESS.

Vocabulary

president	obey	criminal
decision	courts	mistakes
resigned	special privi-	scandal
realized	leges	resolved
Congress	opposite	options
impeach	tried in court	order
block justice	jail	Justice Depart-
burglary	former	ment
to cover it up	found guilty	sue
investigation	foreign	pardon
truth	divided	

One month after taking office, Ford pardoned
Nixon for "all offenses against the United States
which he . . . has committed or may have committed or taken part in" during his presidency (option
d). Students should have done the 1974 Watergate
decision or studied the issue in some other way
before doing this decision. Possibly pertinent to your
discussion are the facts that Ford had not been
elected vice president but had been named by Nixon
to that position; that he became the first nonelected
vice president and president; and that Nixon and
Ford may have agreed on a future pardon prior to
Nixon's resignation.

1974—Supreme Court: What rights do non-English-speaking students have? (Lau Case)

See also 1994—CALIFORNIANS.

Vocabulary

justice	languages	hire
United States	responsibility	native
Supreme Court	falling behind	language
arguments	subjects	agree
education	English-speak-	force
public schools	ing	

Kinney Lau and 1,800 other Chinese-Ameri-
can children sued San Francisco Public Schools for
failing to provide an equal educational opportunity
for Chinese-speaking children. The case was
defeated in federal district and appeals court. In
1974, the Supreme Court decided unanimously in
Lau *v.* Nichols that the children's rights had been

violated under Title VII of the 1964 Civil Rights Act, rather than under the Fourteenth Amendment, as the petitioners had hoped. Although the Court stated that students of limited English proficiency had a right to special treatment, it did not specify what that treatment should be (option *b*). The Court's decision mentioned English as a Second Language (ESL) instruction and bilingual education as options. Two justices wrote that the number of students per language had to be "substantial" (option *d*) before special treatment was warranted.

As a result of the decision, the San Francisco Unified School District began bilingual programs in Chinese, Spanish, and Tagalog (the language groups with the largest populations) and ESL instruction for other limited English proficient students (combination of options *d* and *e*).

The Commissioner of Education issued the Lau Remedies to interpret the Supreme Court's ruling. The office of Civil Rights used the guidelines to measure school districts' compliance with Lau.

1979—American Citizens: What should we do to get our hostages out of Iran?

Vocabulary		
worried	hostages	military bases
confused	shouted	cruel dictator
terrible event	represents	Moslem religious
mob	government	beliefs
culture	protect	religious society
embassy	supporting	fled
capital	Shah	cancer
kidnapped	modernize	medical attention
blindfolds	militant revolu-	criminal
torture	tionaries	imprison
disagreed	opposed	spies
trial	communism	overthrew
immediately		

Of the original 66 hostages, the militants soon released 13 blacks and females. Ten days after the hostages were taken, President Carter froze $8 billion in Iranian assets in banks in the U.S. and throughout the world (choice *j*). The U.S. also deported Iranian students (choice *f*). The U.S. appealed to the U.N., and the Security Council unanimously demanded a return of the hostages. The U.S. arranged for the Shah to go to Panama, and he eventually went to Egypt, where he died in July 1980 (choice *i*). On his death, the militants demanded that the U.S. return his family's assets.

They also demanded that the U.S. cease interference in Iran, unfreeze Iranian assets, cancel all economic sanctions against Iran, and apologize for U.S. actions against Iran. On March 24, 1980, the U.S. sent a military force to rescue the hostages (choice *c*), but the raid was aborted when the helicopters collided in the desert, killing eight and injuring five others. Eventually, the U.S. agreed to and fulfilled most of Iran's conditions (choice *g*). The remaining 52 hostages were released on January 20, 1980 (the day Ronald Reagan was sworn in as president), after 444 days in captivity.

1979—American Citizens: Should we continue to develop nuclear power? (Three Mile Island)

Vocabulary		
citizen	similar	depend
accident	design	foreign
nuclear	construction	oil
power plant	electricity	produce
valve	nuclear power	energy
serious	temporary sites	cheaply
millions	waste	electric bills
gallons	permanent	develop
radioactive	to store	proves
steam	neighbors	disaster
evacuated	hundreds of	radiation
explode	thousands	traffic jams
difficult	in favor of	material

Nuclear power was increasingly popular following the oil crisis of 1973. Three Mile Island threatened the industry's plan for more nuclear plants. Public fears about nuclear power, raised by the incident at Three Mile Island and the 1979 film *The China Syndrome*, led the federal government's Nuclear Regulatory Commission to conduct more thorough research on nuclear plants (option *i*). In the period between 1976 and 1980, the government also increased federal spending on development of alternative energy resources (option *j*). Nationwide, orders for new plants were cancelled (option *c*).

Much of the debate over nuclear power took place at the state and local levels. In Maine and New Hampshire, a series of referendum questions asked voters to shut down existing plants (option *a*). Another concern was storage of nuclear wastes, with most states choosing to pay another state or country to accept nuclear waste (option *g*). Barrels full of nuclear waste have been discovered in the oceans, too (option *h*).

Students should see that this decision has ramifications far beyond the present.

1980—American Citizens: What should we do about the Southeast Asian refugees?

See also 1964—U.S. Congress; 1969—President Nixon.

Vocabulary

citizen	family members	United Nations
health clinics	punished	settle
fleeing violence	political	supporting
civil war	million	refugees
communist	murdered	reasons
accept	hundreds of	imprisonment
economic	thousands	

When the first waves of Southeast Asian refugees ("boat people") arrived in the first asylum camps in 1975, the U.S. made few distinctions (choices *a* and *b*). In the early 1980's, the U.S. continued its policy of accepting refugees but tried to distinguish between economic and political refugees (choice *c*). Beginning in 1980, the U.S. placed a "ceiling" on the number of refugees who could enter the U.S. each year (choice *d*). For example, the "ceiling" for refugee admissions from all countries in 1980 was 231,000. The total number actually admitted was 207,116; of those, 166,700 (80 percent) were Southeast Asian (Lao, Lao highlanders, Khmer, Vietnamese). During the ensuing years, the "ceilings" gradually decreased, but were never met. Although some countries accepted only educated and skilled refugees (choice *e*), the U.S. did not distinguish between them (choice *f*). While the U.S. has accepted the largest number of refugees (51 percent), other destinations have been China (19 percent), Canada and France (7.6 percent each), and Australia (6.7 percent).

1982—American Citizens: Should we approve the Equal Rights Amendment?

See also 1848—Women; 1920—State Legislators.

Vocabulary

state legislature	equal rights	bank account
discussing	in favor of	sexual discrimi-nation
amendment	discrimination	illegal
Constitution	lawyers	treated
Equal Rights Amendment	engineers	drafted
amend	reason	employer
Senate	accepted	military
House of Repre-sentatives	professions	protections
approve	companies	privileges
debating	salaries	divorce
guarantees	promotions	alimony
raises	bosses	ex-husband
arguments	managers	abandons
gender	property	child support
	borrow	
	permission	

The ERA was a simple sentence: "Equality of Rights under the law shall not be denied or abridged by the United States or any state on account of sex." The ERA was first proposed to Congress in 1923, and some version of it had been discussed in every succeeding congressional term until 1972, when the National Organization for Women (NOW) championed it. It passed 30 state legislatures the next year. The ratification deadline was March 1979, but in 1978 the deadline was extended to June 30, 1982. Eventually, 35 states ratified it, but it fell three states short. Polls indicated that a majority of Americans supported it, but conservative majorities in state legislatures were able to defeat it. It was reintroduced to Congress in 1982 but defeated in the House in 1983.

1986—American Citizens: How can we stop the use of illegal drugs?

Vocabulary

citizen	addicts	infected
concerned	cultivation	penalty
drugs	impossible	needles
afford	legalize	representatives
dangerous	illegal	violent
AIDS	expensive	unsafe
commit	educate	dangers

In 1986, the Reagan Administration declared "war on drugs." Under "drug czar" William Simon, the federal government toughened the penalties for drug use (option *c*) and for selling drugs (option *d*).

The government also gave money to the states and cities to hire more police (option *e*) and employed the Coast Guard to stop and search boats suspected of bringing drugs into U.S. territory (option *g*). Private and public sectors increasingly used drug testing of employees (option *n*), with controversy over constitutional limits and civil rights violations.

Outside the U.S., the government has given money, military supplies, and training to drug-producing nations that agree to lower drug production and shipment to the United States. In at least one case (the capture of Panamanian General Manuel Noriega), the U.S. has cut ties to foreign leaders involved in the drug trade (option *l*). Foreign countries contend that the U.S. is not doing enough to stem the demand for drugs. (See also 1987—U.S. Congress). As the Iran-Contra scandal demonstrated, U.S. officials have used money from drug profits for political benefit.

Critics of U.S. drug policy contend that not enough money is spent on educating Americans about the dangers of drugs (option *a*) or on counseling/rehabilitation for drug users (option *b*). Some people in government see profit as the main source of the drug crisis. At the same time as penalties are made tougher for drug trafficking and drug use (option *c*), some Americans support the legalization of drugs such as marijuana (option *i*), in the belief that drug-related violence, inside and outside the U.S., will decline when profits do.

Students could compare this decision with the temperance movement and passage of the Eighteenth and Twenty-first Amendments.

1987—U.S. Congress: What should we do about the Iran-Contra scandal?

Vocabulary

congressperson	trial	appoint
government	million	administration
employees	amendment	survivor
lied	agencies	drug cartels
activities	disagreed	cocaine
advisers	policy	aides
to break the law	convinced	support
deciding	illegal	protect
communist	allowed	truth
rebels	weapons	panel
missiles	enemy	investigate
foreign	impeach	

In contrast to Carter's efforts at friendship with the Sandinistas, Reagan cut aid to the Nicaraguan government. Claiming that Nicaragua was sending Soviet arms to guerrillas in El Salvador, the Reagan administration began supporting the Contras, a small group of counterrevolutionaries and former members of Somoza's National Guard. U.S. aid for the Contras totaled $90 million in 1982–83.

Worried that its war powers were being infringed upon, Congress looked for ways to limit the administration's covert activities in Central America. In 1982, the Boland Amendment (cosponsored by Edward Boland, D-Mass and Tom Harkin, D-Iowa) barred all aid to the Contras by the CIA, the Pentagon, and all other intelligence agencies. Another $24 million was authorized for humanitarian aid in 1984.

In 1984, Congress discovered that the CIA had mined Nicaraguan harbors. Ships from the Soviet Union, Japan, Holland, Panama, and Liberia were damaged by the U.S. mines. Both houses of Congress and the U.N. Security Council passed resolutions condemning this as an act of aggression against Nicaragua. When the World Court issued a similar verdict, the Reagan administration announced that it would not accept World Court jurisdiction in Central America.

Lt. Colonel Oliver North, working for the National Security Council, began to look for ways to finance the Contras without spending tax money. At first, other countries (Saudi Arabia, Taiwan, and Brunei) were convinced to donate money to the Contras. Arms sales were another fundraiser operated by the National Security Council. Initially, the U.S. allowed Israel to sell U.S-made weapons to Iran (for use in their war with Iraq). Eventually, Reagan authorized CIA arms sales to Iran. The profits from these illegal sales were used to fund the Contras and were never reported to Congress. The arms sales were also used as a means of convincing pro-Iranian groups in Lebanon to release U.S. hostages there.

In October 1986, Nicaraguan soldiers downed a Contra supply plane. The only survivor was a U.S. citizen, Eugene Hasenfus, who claimed that the supply route was operated by the CIA. Other people believe that Colombian drug cartels also delivered supplies to the Contras in exchange for permission to fly cocaine shipments into the United States.

When these facts became public knowledge, Reagan was forced to name an investigatory commission to look into what became known as the Iran-Contra scandal (option *e*). The Tower Commission (former Texas Senator John Tower, former Secretary of State Edmund Muskie, and Brent Scowcroft) and both houses of Congress held hearings to determine if the Boland Amendment had been violated and if the president had known about the arms sales. Dramatic testimony from Oliver North, Attorney General Edwin Meese, and other administration officials and government employees led the Tower Commission to conclude that Reagan had not known the details of the National Security Council's creation of international funding for the Contras. Reagan was strongly criticized for being "out of touch" with what members of his administration were doing.

1990—American Citizens: What should we do about Iraq? (Persian Gulf War)

Vocabulary

debts	leader	citizen
disobeyed	opposes	thousand
escaped	oil-producing	royal family
ally	experienced fighters	producing
captured	neighbor	region
boycott	invaded	troops
defend	powerful military	weapons
defeat	peace	oil fields
billions		

The U.S., Britain, France, the U.S.S.R., China, and the European Community immediately condemned Iraq's invasion and set up embargoes and boycotts. The U.N. passed several resolutions establishing economic sanctions and threatening military intervention if Iraq did not withdraw by January 15, 1991 (option *f*). The U.S. sent forces to protect Saudi Arabia (option *c*). A coalition of Western and Arab forces sent support. By December, 90 percent of Iraq's imports and 97 percent of her exports had been stopped, but the economic sanctions did not seem likely to force Iraq's withdrawal. The coalition attacked from January 16 to February 28 (options *a* and *d*). With high casualties on the Iraqi side, Iraq accepted the U.N. resolution establishing terms of a cease-fire and ending the economic sanctions on April 6, 1991. The significance of the action was the international coalition that formed, at U.S. insistence, involving the United Nations, the West, the U.S.S.R. and China, and the Arab states.

1990—American Citizens: Should English be the official language of the United States?

See also 1974—SUPREME COURT.

Vocabulary

legislature	culture	to pass
courts	immigrants	representatives
constitutional amendment	ignore	official
	bilingual	legislature
pro	forbidding	amended
con	citizen	national
translating documents	common	language
	native	foreign

The issue of an official language in the United States goes back to at least 1753, when Benjamin Franklin criticized the widespread use of German in Pennsylvania. Although the U.S. has never had an official language, many Americans assume that English is the country's official language. Public support for making English the official language seems to vary with the state of the national economy and with waves of immigration.

The latest push for an official English policy began in 1981, when Senator S.I. Hayakawa of California proposed an English Language Amendment to the U.S. Constitution. Sixteen such amendments were proposed in Congress between 1981 and 1990. Some of the proposed amendments have declared English the official language of the United States, leaving interpretation to Congress and the courts. Other versions have mandated that the federal, state, and local governments use English only, with some exceptions for health and educational purposes.

Although official language amendments have never reached a vote in the Congress, many state and some local governments have passed measures promoting English to official language status. By 1992, 17 states had adopted some form of official English legislation. Ten states (Arkansas, Indiana, Illinois, Kentucky, Mississippi, North Carolina, North Dakota, South Carolina, Tennessee, and Virginia) have passed official English statutes. Six states (Alabama, Arizona, California, Colorado, Florida, and Nebraska) have passed constitutional amendments. Hawaii declared itself officially bilingual (English and Native Hawaiian) in 1978 (option *b*). Since most of these measures leave interpretation to legislatures and the courts, there are ongoing legal battles over the rights of minority language users to use a language other than English in the domains of public education, courts, social services, public safety, and the workplace. One reaction to English only and official English legislation is the English Plus movement, which promotes use of English and other languages while denying the need for an official language amendment (option *b*).

This decision provides an opportunity for students to consider the linguistic diversity in their families, community, and classrooms. Students can investigate state language policy and proposed national plans (during the 1996 presidential elections, several presidential candidates declared support for English-only or official English legislation). They can consider the implications of the options proposed in this decision for their own state. James Crawford's book *Language Loyalties: A Sourcebook on the Official English Controversy* is an excellent resource for teachers who wish to explore this issue at different points in American history. Finally, you may wish to compare the situation in the United States with policy in other multilingual nations such as Canada, South Africa, and Australia.

1992—U.S. Congress: Should the U.S. sign a free trade agreement with Canada and Mexico? (NAFTA)

Vocabulary

member	pollute	signed
Congress	guarantee	expensive
president	foreign markets	labor unions
negotiating	import taxes	hire
trade	companies	benefit
neighbors	factories	minimum wage
approve	labor	strict
agreement	costs	competition
vote	consumers	environmentalists
products		

Presidents Bush and Clinton pushed the North American Free Trade Agreement hard in order to win congressional approval. Fearing loss of U.S. jobs and environmental damage, labor unions and environmentalists lobbied Congress to reject the bill, pending changes in certain sections of the agreement. Despite this opposition, both Houses of Congress approved NAFTA by a wide margin.

The consensus was that regional trading blocks were developing in Europe and the Pacific Rim, and that NAFTA provided favorable conditions for continued U.S. economic dominance of North America. Negotiations soon began for the inclusion

of Chile, with the idea of eventually including all of the Americas in the free-trade pact.

The agreement went into effect January 1, 1994. The collapse of the Mexican economy and political instability there, and the continued push to strengthen labor and environmental protection, should be considered.

1993—U.S. Congress: Should Congress make it harder to buy handguns? (Brady Bill)

Vocabulary

congressperson	strict	accidentally
vote	registration	suicides
approves	amendment	trained
bill	Constitution	drowning
difficult	right	self-defense
handguns	military	protect
arguments	hunting	criminals
con	target shooting	attack
pro	dangerous	steal
law-abiding	accidents	crime rate
gun control laws	fifth highest	unregistered

The "Brady Bill" passed. It requires a five-day waiting period prior to possession of a handgun. During the waiting period, a background check on the customer's criminal and mental health record is to be made through the police. Purchase is to be denied if the person was previously convicted of a felony or if there is a public record of mental illness. The Brady Bill was passed over the objections of the National Rifle Association, which lobbied hard for unrestricted freedom to own guns. This was the first setback for the NRA. Since passage of the bill, its constitutionality has been challenged in a few state courts.

In 1997, the Supreme Court decided that states could not be compelled to pay for costs of the background checks, but the waiting period and ability to deny handgun purchase were upheld as constitutional.

1994—Californians: Should California help people who come here illegally to live?

See 1948—U.S. FARM WORKERS.

Vocabulary

resident	taxes	disease
elections	federal	citizens
voters	approve	communicate
decision	referendum	enforce
illegal immi-	public services	restaurants
grants	economy	cause trouble
thousands	labor	obey
permission	picked	populous
attend	epidemic	similar
border	health services	

In November 1994, California voters passed the referendum question Proposition 187, with 60 percent of the voters in favor and 40 percent opposed. Opponents of the measure filed injunctions in the state courts, blocking it at least temporarily. Both sides promised to continue working for their beliefs. It seems likely that the issue will spread to other border states, and perhaps be decided in the U.S. Supreme Court. The sentiment behind Proposition 187 motivated federal authorities to strengthen the U.S. border patrol on the U.S.–Mexican border. California Governor Pete Wilson admitted his family had employed an illegal domestic worker, but went on to seek the Republican nomination for the presidency in 1996, basing much of his campaign on a strong anti-illegal immigrant stance. Anti-immigrant and anti-Latino violence rose in California following passage of Proposition 187.

Students should consider this decision in light of the 1948 decision by farm owners to bring Mexican workers here, and of the role of Mexican labor in the U.S. during World War II. Students can take roles of farm owners and other employers, as well as legal and illegal immigrants.

Thematic Index for Volumes 1 and 2

Notes

Notes

Share Your Bright Ideas with Us!

We want to hear from you! Your valuable comments and suggestions will help us meet your current and future classroom needs.

Your name_____Date_____

School name_____Phone_____

School address_____

Grade level taught_____Subject area(s) taught_____Average class size_____

Where did you purchase this publication?_____

Was your salesperson knowledgeable about this product?   Yes_____   No_____

What monies were used to purchase this product?

____School supplemental budget   ____Federal/state funding   ____Personal

Please "grade" this Walch publication according to the following criteria:

Quality of service you received when purchasing ....A   B   C   D   F
Ease of use..A   B   C   D   F
Quality of content..A   B   C   D   F
Page layout ....A   B   C   D   F
Organization of material ....A   B   C   D   F
Suitability for grade level ....A   B   C   D   F
Instructional value...A   B   C   D   F

COMMENTS:_____

_____

What specific supplemental materials would help you meet your current—or future—instructional needs?

_____

Have you used other Walch publications? If so, which ones?_____

May we use your comments in upcoming communications?   ___Yes   ___No

Please **FAX** this completed form to **207-772-3105**, or mail it to:

Product Development, J. Weston Walch, Publisher, P.O. Box 658, Portland, ME 04104-0658

We will send you a **FREE GIFT** as our way of thanking you for your feedback. **THANK YOU!**